Paddling
Cape Cod

EVENDEN '99

Paddling Cape Cod

A Coastal Explorer's Guide

Shirley and Fred Bull

Illustrations by Phyllis Evenden

Foreword by Nancy Church,
Cape Cod Museum of Natural History

BACK COUNTRY

BACKCOUNTRY GUIDES
WOODSTOCK, VERMONT

With time, access points may change, and road numbers, signs, and landmarks referred to in this book may be altered. If you find that such changes have occurred, please let the author and publisher know, so that corrections may be made in future editions. Other comments and suggestions are also welcome. Address all correspondence to:

Backcountry Editor
The Countryman Press
P.O. Box 748
Woodstock, VT 05091

Library of Congress Cataloging-in-Publication Data
Bull, Shirley.
    Paddling Cape Cod : a coastal explorer's guide / Shirley and Fred Bull ; illustrations by Phyllis Evenden.
       p. cm.
       ISBN 0-88150-441-6 (alk. paper)
       1. Sea kayaking—Massachusetts—Cape Cod—Guidebooks. 2. Canoes and canoeing—Massachusetts—Cape Cod—Guidebooks. 3. Cape Cod (Mass.)—Guidebooks. I. Bull, Fred. II. Title.

GV776.M42 C362 2000   99-087152

Cover and text design by Faith Hague
Cover photographs by Kim Grant
Interior photographs by the authors
Maps by Paul Woodward, © 2000 The Countryman Press
Illustrations © 2000 by Phyllis Evenden

Published by Backcountry Guides
A division of The Countryman Press
P.O. Box 748
Woodstock, VT 05091

Distributed by W. W. Norton & Company, Inc.
500 Fifth Avenue
New York, NY 10110

Printed in the United States of America

10 9 8 7

Acknowledgments

WE WISH TO thank all of our patrons and friends who helped make this guide a reality. Their continued patronage over the years and their interest in paddling new and uncharted routes have led us to explore every tidal river, meandering creek, salt-marsh rivulet, and sheltered bay on Cape Cod.

The allure of Cape Cod's waterways is not measured in miles, nor by class or degree of difficulty, but by the natural wonders that one encounters, whether paddling a tiny creek on Barnstable Great Marsh, or crossing to an island on Little Pleasant Bay. We hope this guide not only introduces you to some of the best paddling spots on Cape Cod, but also inspires and excites you to explore new territory.

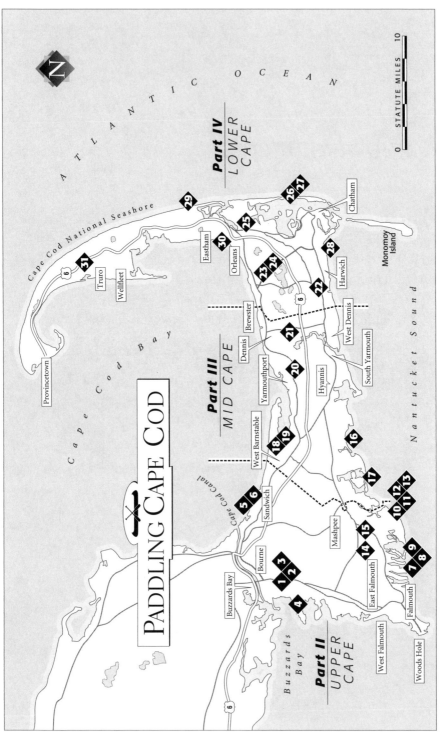

PADDLING CAPE COD

Part II
UPPER CAPE

Part III
MID CAPE

Part IV
LOWER CAPE

ATLANTIC OCEAN

Cape Cod National Seashore

Cape Cod Bay

Buzzards Bay

Nantucket Sound

Cape Cod Canal

Provincetown

Truro
Wellfleet

Eastham
Orleans

Brewster
Dennis
Yarmouthport
Hyannis
West Dennis
South Yarmouth
West Yarmouth
Harwich
Chatham

Monomoy Island

West Barnstable

Sandwich
Bourne

Buzzards Bay

Mashpee
East Falmouth
West Falmouth
Falmouth
Woods Hole

0   STATUTE MILES   10

Contents

Foreword

GEOGRAPHICALLY SPEAKING, Cape Cod is an island, with more than 1,000 miles of shoreline and replete with bays, inlets, estuaries, rivers, and creeks. Three very different bodies of water shape the coastline: Cape Cod Bay, Nantucket Sound, and the Atlantic Ocean, all with varying conditions and features. In addition, there are more than 350 freshwater ponds.

For much of the year it is possible to explore one of these ponds, walk an isolated stretch of shoreline, or follow a marsh side trail without seeing another person. However, as the popularity of the Cape grows, it is becoming increasingly difficult to experience any degree of solitude, especially in summer. It is a challenge to find those special places, far from the buzz of human activity, where the only sounds may be the cry of a tern or waves lapping against the shore. Local knowledge and a sense of adventure are required to discover those quiet places away from other people. Paddling is an ideal way to reconnect with nature, escape the crowds, and explore long-forgotten parts of the Cape, and this first guidebook to paddling Cape Cod provides all the information you will need to get started.

As director of education for the Cape Cod Museum of Natural History, my goal is to provide opportunities for people to access those special places, in order to fulfill the museum's mission: To encourage appreciation and advance understanding of our natural environment through discovery and learning. Paddling provides a means for people to explore the natural world from a different perspective. Close encounters with osprey, great blue heron, and a variety of rare and endangered shorebirds are all possible with canoes and kayaks. Traveling through the marsh creeks, one has the chance to watch the mud come alive with fiddler and horseshoe crabs, killifish, and snails. A kingfisher may swoop down to capture a minnow in its beak, just inches from the bow.

Fred and Shirley Bull of Cape Cod Coastal Canoe and Kayak created the first commercial venture that leads paddling tours on the Cape in 1993. Since then they have introduced hundreds of people—including many museum groups interested in natural history—to unexplored areas from one end of the Cape to the other. Many of their trips focus on places accessible only by canoe or kayak, keeping them relatively pristine. In this book, they share with you many of their favorite paddling locations, as well as directions, parking, and tide information to help get you under way. Details such as distance, conditions, accessibility, and rules and regulations offer the kind of local information that can save you from a disastrous experience.

This book comes at a time when more and more people are looking for ways to get back to nature. Ecotourism is on the rise, and canoeing and kayaking are more popular than ever. Uniquely, Fred and Shirley combine paddling experience with a well-developed knowledge of natural history. This book will not only guide you to the right location but provides a general overview of each area, along with accounts of the habitats and types of wildlife you are likely to encounter. Knowing what to look for can greatly enhance observations on any outdoor trip. I'm pleased to recommend this excellent guide, which will expose people to special places and lead them to discover the true nature of Cape Cod.

Nancy Church
Director of Education
Cape Cod Museum of Natural History

PART I

Setting Out on the Water

CAPE COD, a peninsula extending from the mainland of Massachusetts, is surrounded by the sea, with Cape Cod Bay to the north, Nantucket Sound and Vineyard Sound to the south, Buzzards Bay to the west, and the Atlantic Ocean to the east. The Cape Cod Canal, which severed the Cape's connections with the mainland in 1914, runs east and west. In addition, Cape Cod is dotted with more than 500 freshwater and saltwater ponds and lakes. This abundance of water offers the paddler numerous opportunities to explore saltwater bays, inlets, marshes, rivers, and coastal ponds, as well as freshwater marshes and glacial kettle ponds. You can experience diverse habitats by putting in

These paddlers have a calm day
for their open water crossing.

at a freshwater pond or river, following it to the sea, and taking out on a barrier beach.

Paddling Cape Cod's coastal waterways is the best way to see its natural beauty and to explore areas accessible only by canoe or kayak. While on the water you may happen upon a great blue heron stalking its prey, or an osprey about to stoop for its dinner. Below the surface you'll see prehistoric horseshoe crabs and gregarious hermit crabs scurrying by in the ever-changing tidal zone.

Coastal paddling offers something that cannot be found on a river or lake—water that flows both ways, eliminating the need for one vehicle at the put-in and another at the takeout. Whether you are a novice or an expert paddler, Cape Cod's waterways offer something for everyone: quiet water for the birder and nature enthusiast, wind-driven surf for the more adventurous.

For many years now we have explored Cape Cod's coastal environs by boat, observing and learning about the rich array of plants and animals that live here. This guide is a culmination of our experience. It is not just a guide of *where* to paddle, but an invitation to paddle with all your senses sharpened—to see, hear, and smell, and most importantly, to appreciate the natural wonders of Cape Cod.

Before we describe our favorite places to paddle, how to make a trip go smoothly, and what might be seen while out on the water, there are a few things that are helpful to know. Paddling is not without its hazards, and we encourage you to be well prepared and cautious, and to use your best judgment at all times.

Tides and Currents

Coastal paddling requires that you plan your trip according to the tides. Too many novice paddlers set out unaware of the tides and find themselves up against a 5-knot current, which may be intensified by a 15-mph head wind that causes waves to swell and break over the bow; the inevitable result is exhaustion and frustration. Others set out to explore the back marshes of tidal creeks and end up high and dry, and find themselves poling out (if possible), or waiting 6 hours for the incoming tide.

Coastal paddling means exploring tidal creeks, rivers, bays, and any other interesting little inlet just around the bend. Sea kayakers on the open ocean also need to work with tides for maximum enjoyment and safety; however, coastal paddlers are more at the mercy of the tides because many areas cannot be navigated at low water. A little knowledge of how tides and currents work will result in much more enjoyable and successful excursions.

The tide goes through two complete cycles on the Cape each day, which means there are two high tides and two low tides approximately every 24 hours. Twice a month, during the full and new moons, the high tide can be dramatically higher and the low tides much lower than normal. As the water level changes along the coast, it also changes in coastal bays. The up and down motion causes the change in tide height (vertical), and the in and out motion causes tidal currents (horizontal). A tidal current flowing into a bay or estuary is called a *flood current;* when it flows out, it is called an *ebb current.* The time between flood and ebb, when little or no current is flowing, is called *slack water.*

How quickly the water flows in and out of embayments is determined by the shape and depths of the embayment, the number of tributaries it has, and the variation in topography of the surrounding area. The tide may be at its high point at the entrance to the bay or river but back in the creeks and marshes near its low point and still coming in.

It is important to know how to determine when to launch your boat, how long you might have to explore an area before you need to think about turning around, and how to use the flow of the tide to your

green-backed heron

advantage. Most of the tours in this guide are on salt water, thus you will need to consult a tide chart and use the launch times we have provided at the beginning of each tour description. Over the years, we have spent many hours "just sitting on the water," charting the flow of the tides in numerous areas to determine the best times to paddle various routes. All of our trips allow for ample time to stop and rest, swim, or beachcomb. But you will need to watch for a changing tide for your return trip. This may all seem rather calculating for an otherwise carefree paddle, but there is plenty of time for a leisurely trip both ways, as long as you launch and reach your destination as planned.

To simplify the calculation we have used the timing of the Boston tide as the marker for all saltwater trips. Most local newspapers provide tide information and list the Boston tide. This information is also readily available through daily weather reports on the television, radio, and the Internet; or you can purchase a current copy of the *Eldridge Tide and Pilot Book,* which includes tide information for the entire Northeast.

The following illustration shows how to plan your tour using a tide chart and the launch times we have provided.

Sample Tide Chart for Boston, Massachusetts
Local Daylight Time

		HIGH		**LOW**		**HIGH**		**LOW**	
Date	Day	Time	ft.	Time	ft.	Time	ft.	Time	ft.
09/11/1999	Sat	00:35	10.93	06:47	-0.48	13:01	10.49	19:05	-0.26
09/12/1999	Sun	01:19	10.67	07:28	-0.21	13:42	10.41	19:50	-0.10
09/13/1999	Mon	02:03	10.30	08:10	0.17	14:22	10.24	20:34	0.17
09/14/1999	Tue	02:46	9.87	08:52	0.61	15:04	9.99	21:19	0.51
09/15/1999	Wed	03:32	9.40	09:35	1.07	15:48	9.69	22:06	0.88
09/16/1999	Thu	04:20	8.94	10:22	1.52	16:35	9.40	22:56	1.22
09/17/1999	Fri	05:12	8.55	11:12	1.89	17:27	9.16	23:50	1.48
09/18/1999	Sat	06:07	8.29	12:05	2.12	18:21	9.04		

Example: If you wanted to paddle from Stage Harbor to Hardings Beach Point on Thursday, September 16, 1999, you would first look at the launch times listed at the beginning of that tour. It would read:

Launch Time: On low; 1 hour before Boston low. Tide turns at Harding Beach 2 hours after launch time.

As indicated, you would need to launch 1 hour before Boston low (shown as 10:22 AM on the tide chart for that particular day). Thus, you would need to get under way by 9:30 AM, and out to Hardings Beach Point before the tide turned and began to come in through the channel about 2 hours later, which would be around 11:30 AM. Basically, this is how to use launch times information for all listed trips. You can adjust your breaks to accommodate your personal paddling speed and any places you choose to stop en route. The launch times are for your convenience in planning a safe and successful trip. However, you may choose to ignore this advice and find paddling against the current a most challenging and exhilarating experience!

All tours in this guide are gauged for 3½ to 4 hours of leisurely paddling at a rate of about 2 miles per hour. If you wish to shorten your trip, and still be paddling with the tide in both directions, add the amount of time you wish to shorten the trip to your launch time. To lengthen your trip, subtract the additional time from your launch time. Use this rule within reason, of course, based on your knowledge of when the tides will turn. Please note that any tide chart is only a close approximation of tide times. Good or bad weather, and high- or low-pressure areas occurring hundreds of miles and days away can influence tidal cycles.

Most launch sites are small and have limited parking, thus we have built a half-hour buffer into each trip to allow for unloading your boat, organizing your gear, finding a place to park, and so on. Using the example above, you could launch as late as 10:00 AM and still make the tide.

Maps

The maps in this book are intended to help you locate the launch location and get a good idea of the tour you are about to take. They are not meant, however, to substitute for the more detailed United States Geological Survey (USGS) maps that we recommend at the beginning of each chapter. USGS maps are generally available at local outdoor shops, boat outfitters, and travel bookstores. If you are an inexperienced paddler and are going without a guide, if you're unfamiliar with the area, or if you are out for more than just a short paddle around a bay, we urge you to pick up the appropriate USGS quadrangles and take them along with you in a waterproof plastic bag.

Equipment

Coastal paddling does not require specialized high-tech gear. Any boat longer than 16 feet would have a hard time negotiating the narrow, winding creeks, and any open vessel shorter than 10 feet may have difficulty in the choppy waters of open bays, all encountered in coastal paddling. A recreational canoe or kayak is ideal for the tours in this guide. The primary equipment required is a boat, a paddle, and a personal flotation device (PFD).

If you are new to paddling, try renting or borrowing a boat before investing in something that may not be what you need. The more boats you try, the better educated you will be. Designers have done wonders to accommodate the needs of the generalist canoeist or kayaker with comfortable, durable, stable, and inexpensive boats that perform just as well on a lake as they do on a calm sea. There are as many manufacturers of boats as there are colors; the boats come in all sizes, materials, shapes, and prices. There are solo, tandem, and multiperson boats, and a boat to match every niche in every habitat. Check the resource section at the end of this book for more advice on boat suppliers and rentals.

Paddles are such personal items that care should be taken when selecting one. Like boats, paddles come in an array of sizes, materials, and shapes. Form follows function. For recreational canoeing you will appreciate a longer, narrower blade with rounded edges at the tip and a pear grip for comfort. Kayak paddles are determined by your height, the boat's length and width, your paddling speed, and where you will be paddling. Depending on your budget and paddling needs, you can choose between wooden, graphite, fiberglass, aluminum, or plastic paddles. All will work, although one will best suit your paddling requirements. A good outdoor equipment store can give you excellent advice on these finer points.

A personal flotation device (PFD) is the most important equipment you will purchase. They do save lives. They are a must, both by law and common sense. There are two sets of laws regulating PFDs. The U.S. Coast Guard requires that you must have at least one Type I, II, III, or IV PFD aboard your canoe or kayak for each person in the boat. Massachusetts law goes further and requires that a Type I, II, or III PFD must be *worn* by all canoe and kayak occupants, at all times, between September 15 and May 15. *Children under the age of 12 must wear a Type I, II, or III PFD on all vessels, at all times of the year.* It is extremely important that the child's PFD be the right size—too large and it could slip off. If you are paddling with a child, wear your PFD not only to set a good example, but also because you will need to first save yourself in order to save your child.

Canoeists and kayakers generally wear Type III PFDs (flotation aid vest type), which are comfortable and come in many styles, materials, colors, and prices. They will all work as long as you buy the correct size and wear it. They will do you no good if stowed in the hatch or under the seat.

Once you obtain the three primary requirements—boat, paddle, and PFD—you will find a plethora of equipment and gadgets available to the paddler, from bilge pumps to dry suits. A few of them are necessities, others are just nice to have.

Clothing

First of all, regardless of time of year, remember to dress for the water temperature, not the air temperature! A sunny day in spring with an air temperature of 70 degrees could still mean water temperatures in the low 40s, and sitting in a kayak attired in shorts would be quite chilly. For cold-weather paddling you need to maintain a balance between the heat your body produces and the heat your body loses. The best way to do this is to layer. The basic concept behind layering is that several layers of lightweight, insulating, moisture-wicking clothing are more effective and versatile for maintaining body temperature than a single layer of heavy insulation. Multiple layers of clothing will trap warm air and make it more difficult for outside cool air currents to reach your skin and rob your body of heat. And while paddling hard and working up a sweat, layers will allow evaporation to occur without losing precious body heat. Most heat loss in humans occurs through the head; wearing a hat is critical to staying warm.

Warm-weather paddling clothing is also dictated by water, not air, temperature. Dress in lightweight, light-colored layers that can be easily removed and stowed away when not needed. A hat with a brim is critical in warm weather to prevent sunstroke. Remember, while out on the water you are totally exposed to the sun's harmful rays, and protective clothing, a hat, and sunglasses are just as important as a good sunscreen lotion.

Safety

Coastal water, unlike white water and the open sea, provides a relatively calm environment, the weather conditions tempered by the shallows and the shoreline. However, don't be lulled into complacency. Know your abilities and limitations. You are ultimately responsible for your own actions and safety. The most important precautionary measure you can take is to always wear your PFD (see Equipment).

Be proactive and prepared. Plan your trip in advance, and read the tide charts to determine if the route you have chosen will work with the tides. Gather local knowledge, such as that of a swift current through a channel, which may impede your passage, or low water that may force you into boat channels with jet skiers and powerboaters (kayaks and canoes are nothing but speed bumps to powerboats). A big wake from a powerboat can quickly swamp or capsize a canoe or kayak. Although human-powered boats have the right-of-way, it is not wise to challenge a powerboat—it may be that they cannot see you low in the water (a kayaker cannot be picked up on radar).

Whether paddling with friends or by yourself, it is advisable to file a trip plan with someone before you go, describing whom you are traveling with, the kind of boats and their colors, your proposed route and launch location, and the time you expect to return.

Paddling safe means being aware of potential hazards and how to avoid them. The fickleness of Cape Cod weather can mean that a clear, calm day can change into a dangerous situation—strong winds preceding a squall line turning tranquil water into whitecapped, 2-foot waves—in a matter of minutes. Sudden thunderstorms are always possible during the hot and humid summer months. Listen to current weather reports before you depart, and learn to read the clouds so you are not taken by surprise and can seek safety in sufficient time. If you are caught out on the water during a lightning storm, it is important that you not be the tallest object around, so try to lay low in your boat.

Hypothermia is probably responsible for more paddling deaths than any other single cause. Extensive information about hypothermia, including the different stages, symptoms, and reactions, as well as prevention, is available in any first-aid guide. Simply stated, hypothermia is best prevented by applying common sense. Disaster can be avoided by using good judgment, knowing your limits, wearing appropriate clothing for cold and wet conditions, and maintaining good physical fitness.

Another threat to paddlers is overexposure to the sun's ultraviolet (UV) rays; this is a danger both in summer and winter. Water can reflect up to 85 percent of the sun's damaging rays. Be safe in the sun by keeping skin exposure to a minimum when the sun's rays are the most intense, between 10:00 AM and 3:00 PM; liberally apply, and reapply every 2 hours, a sunscreen with a sun protection factor (SPF) of at least 15; wear appropriate clothing, including a hat and long-sleeve shirt; wear UV-protected sunglasses to filter out the sun's harmful rays; and beware of cloudy and foggy days, for up to 80 percent of the sun's rays can penetrate through the haze. Always carry plenty of drinking water, and drink frequently during strenuous paddling in order to avoid dehydration.

Weather

Cape Cod's location, surrounded by water on all sides, influences the moderate weather we enjoy year-round. We benefit from the warming effects of the ocean in winter and its cooling breezes in summer. Spring here begins late and brings more cool and cloudy days, but on the other end, autumn arrives late, lingers longer, and we don't usually get a frost until late October.

With such a perfect climate, paddling on Cape Cod is three-season recreation and can even extend through winter, if you have the proper clothing and equipment. Winter is a wonderful time to paddle—you'll find crisp, clear days, your only companions seals and ducks.

There is no one overall weather forecast for the Cape. You could be paddling Nauset Marsh in Eastham on a "three-B day"—bright, blue, and beautiful—while an hour's drive away at Sandwich Harbor it might be raining. Check weather forecasts for specific towns, rather than an all-inclusive Cape Cod forecast from an off-Cape radio or television station.

For your safety, understand weather terms and patterns: low pressure, high pressure, cold fronts, warm fronts, thermals, or northeasters. Listen to wind reports; in the summer months prevailing winds are from the southwest and in winter from the northwest. The most damaging winds are from the northeast, which are due to oceanic storms, and usually blow for at least 3 days. Watch the clouds. Learn the six basic types of clouds and what they mean, how are they changing, and the effect they will have on you. Be an observer of nature.

Knowledge of weather patterns, winds, and clouds will assist you in making your paddling trip one to remember, not one you'd rather forget.

Public/Private Access

Never before in the Cape's history has public access to the coast been more restricted, yet at the same time more coveted. At the turn of the 20th century, the Cape's residents built their houses away from the perils of the sea. Today, available coastal building lots are rare and few and, if available, priced beyond the budget of most Cape Codders. Many "quaint Cape Cod cottages" have been replaced with sprawling, ostentatious symbols of wealth.

We may no longer have shore access in many places. However, once on the water we are all entitled to beach access in accordance with the Massachusetts Public Trust Doctrine, which states that the public has the right to fish, fowl, and navigate on tidal flats (the area between the high- and low-tide lines). Nonetheless, respect the rights of the owners of private property and do not enter without their permission. If you carry a fishing pole with you at all times, your legal right to walk the intertidal zone is protected. While on the water, stay clear of buoys marking commercial shellfish grants. Remember, this is where and how many people earn their living providing us with succulent morsels from the sea!

All of the launch areas described in this book are owned by either the town, state, or federal goverment and are opened to the public from mid-June through Labor Day. When this guide went to press, all information regarding parking and fees was up-to-date; however, you may wish to check with the local Town Harbormaster or town hall for any changes to the rules and regulations. (Phone numbers and addresses are listed in the Resource Appendix.)

Please be a good steward of this fragile and beautiful environment. Obey the signs posted to protect nesting birds and the tender beach grass planted to halt dune erosion. Park only in designated areas so as not to disturb vegetation. Carry out whatever you bring in, and make a difference by picking up after others who were not as thoughtful as you.

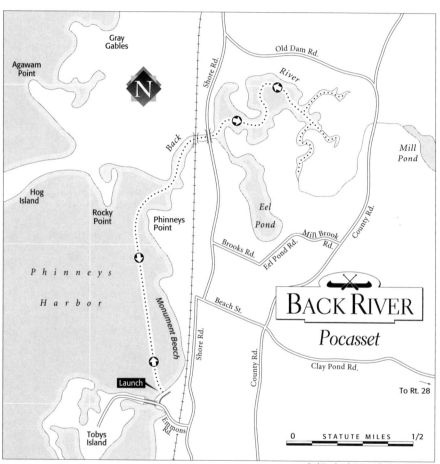

Gray
Gables

Agawam
Point

N

Shore Rd.

Old Dam Rd.

River

Mill
Pond

Back

Hog
Island

Rocky
Point

Phinneys
Point

Eel
Pond

Mill Brook
Rd.

County Rd.

P h i n n e y s

H a r b o r

Brooks Rd.

Eel Pond Rd.

Beach St.

Monument Beach

BACK RIVER

Pocasset

Launch

Shore Rd.

County Rd.

Clay Pond Rd.

To Rt. 28

Tobys
Island

Emmons Rd.

0   STATUTE MILES   1/2

PART II
Upper Cape Paddling Tours

1. Back River, Pocasset (Town of Bourne)

Maps:
> USGS Onset Quadrangle
> USGS Pocasset Quadrangle

Launch location: Monument Beach, at the end of Emmons Road
Habitats: Bay, salt marsh
Length of trip: 3½ hours
Type of trip: Round-trip paddle
Paddling distance: 4 miles
Paddling conditions: Open bay into protected salt marsh

A kayaker enters the Back River

Current: Flood in/ebb out. Tide turns in Back River 2 hours 15 minutes after launch.

Launch time: On high, 3 hours 30 minutes before Boston high

Permits, fees, parking: No permits or fees required to park or launch. Large paved lot.

Facilities: Toilets (seasonal), telephone, seasonal take-out restaurant

Handicap access: Paved ramp

Directions to launch: From Bourne Bridge rotary, drive 1.8 miles south on MA 28, turn right onto Clay Pond Road, and go 1.3 miles to its intersection with County Road. Continue across the intersection onto Beach Street, go 0.5 mile, and bear left after a stop sign onto shore road. Continue 0.5 mile, take a right onto Emmons Road, and follow the road into the parking lot for Monument Beach.

The Tour

The Back River, aptly named for its location "back" of Phinneys Harbor, is a transition zone between the dry uplands of the Bourne Woodlands Conservation Area and the salt water of Phinneys Harbor. It is also an ideal location if you are seeking solitude, with no powerboats and very few paddlers!

Begin this trip by heading north along Monument Beach. After weaving your way through the moored boats you will reach Phinneys Point. You are now at the mouth of the Back River. Large glacial erratics (boulders transported here by glaciers) lie just under the water's surface, so keep a lookout for the pillows formed as water surges over these submerged rocks. At the base of the boulders you will see bright red clumps of red beard sponges. As you enter the Back River the current will quicken, and you'll want to line yourself up to pass under the two bridges. The first is a railroad bridge, where you may encounter a number of ropes hanging down and children jumping off the bridge. Avoid them! Once under the second bridge the current will slow. Bear left as the river forks and paddle into the salt marsh. Follow the tidal current into the marsh as far as your boat will allow. Set against the lush green of the salt marsh you may see nesting osprey, stalking great blue heron, elegant great egret or their smaller cousin the snowy egret. Below

The Back River is almost free of motorboat traffic.

the surface, blue crab, shrimp, herring, and mummichog swim or crawl about.

One hour after entering the marsh the tide will begin to ebb. Wait for the tide to change, because passing under the bridges is nearly impossible beforehand. Retrace your route back to the launch.

Note: If the wind is too strong to paddle the Phinneys Harbor leg of this trip, don't despair, for there is an alternative (see Tour 3, Pocasset River).

2. *Tobys Island to Wings Neck, Pocasset (Town of Bourne)*

Maps:
   USGS Onset Quadrangle
Launch location: Monument Beach, at the end of Emmons Road
Habitats: Glacial moraine bay, sandy island
Length of trip: 3½ hours
Type of trip: Round-trip paddle
Paddling distance: 4½ miles
Paddling conditions: Flat water on an open bay
Current: Ebb out/flood in. Tide turns at west end of Wings Neck
   1 hour 30 minutes after launch.

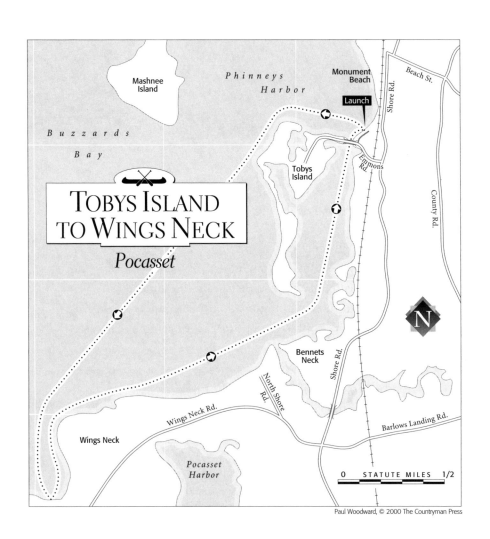

Mashnee
Island

P h i n n e y s
H a r b o r

Monument
Beach

Beach St.

Launch

Shore Rd.

B u z z a r d s

B a y

Tobys
Island

Emmons
Rd.

County Rd.

TOBYS ISLAND
TO WINGS NECK

Pocasset

N

Bennets
Neck

Shore Rd.

North Shore
Rd.

Wings Neck Rd.

Barlows Landing Rd.

Wings Neck

Pocasset
Harbor

0   STATUTE MILES   1/2

Launch time: On low, 3 hours before Boston low. Go as early as possible to avoid paddling into a strong wind.

Permits, fees, parking: No parking permits required or fee to launch. Large paved lot.

Facilities: Toilets, telephone

Handicap access: Paved ramp

Directions to launch: From the Bourne Bridge rotary, go 1.8 miles south on MA 28, then turn right onto Clay Pond Road. Drive 1.3 miles to its intersection with County Road, continue across onto Beach Street, and go another 0.5 mile to a stop sign. Turn left onto Shore Road and continue 0.5 mile; turn right onto Emmons Road, which you follow to the Monument Beach parking lot.

The Tour

Seventeen thousand years ago, two enormous sheets of ice, each more than a mile high, collided along what is now the western shore of Cape Cod. Today, the piles of huge glacial erratics—boulders left when the ice melted—cause this side of the Cape to resemble coastal Maine. However, not all of the geologic features are natural. In the 1930s, the islands of Mashnee and Hog became a peninsula when material dredged from the deepening and widening of the Cape Cod Canal was deposited between the two islands. The canal work affected Phinneys Harbor in other ways; the once plentiful oyster is scarcely found today. To begin your tour, launch alongside the boat ramp. You will notice that there is no water under the bridge connecting Tobys Island to the mainland, but don't worry, by the time you return there will be more than enough to complete your trip.

As you start out along the northern shore of Tobys Island you will see many sailboats at their moorings. The prevailing southwest winds of summer funnel up Buzzards Bay and make for many excellent sailing days, but some tough paddling ones. The best time to plan your trip (provided the tide is favorable) is as early in the morning as possible. If the wind comes up (and by midmorning it usually does), you will be on the return leg with a following wind.

Jingle, slipper, cardita, and other shells are common along the shore.

Once you round the northwest tip of Tobys Island, point your bow to the southwest. Two miles away is Wings Neck. On a calm day the paddle across the open water to Wings Cove is glorious. Depending on the season, you could be gliding alongside loons, grebes, brants, eiders, seals, bluefish, or striped bass. Off to the west, ships and boats of all types and sizes enter or exit the canal.

Once on Wings Neck, stop for a break and take in the panoramic view. Be sure to stay within the intertidal zone so that you don't trespass on private property. When the tide changes and begins to come in, or flood, you can return. Follow along the shore of Wings Neck, keeping the shore to your right, until you reach Bennets Neck. From there continue north to the takeout at Monument Beach.

3. *Pocasset River, Pocasset (Town of Bourne)*

Maps:
   USGS Onset Quadrangle
   USGS Pocasset Quadrangle
Launch location: Shore Road Town Landing, on west side of Shore Road bridge.

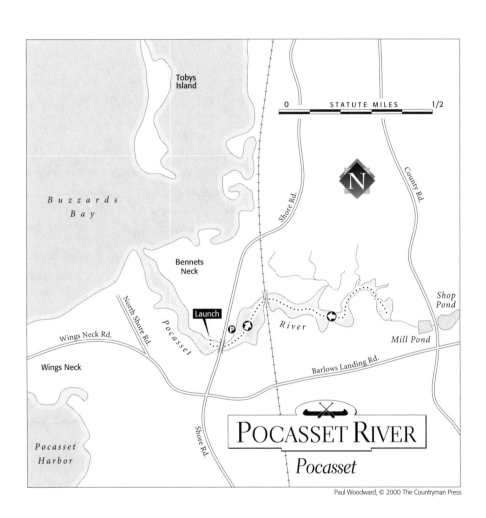

Tobys
Island

STATUTE MILES

0 · · · · 1/2

N

County Rd.

*Buzzards
Bay*

Shore Rd.

Shop
Pond

Bennets
Neck

Pocasset

Launch

P

River

Mill Pond

North Shore Rd.

Wings Neck Rd.

Barlows Landing Rd.

Wings Neck

*Pocasset
Harbor*

Shore Rd.

POCASSET RIVER

Pocasset

Habitats: Salt marsh

Length of trip: 2½ hours

Type of trip: Round-trip paddle

Paddling distance: 2 miles

Paddling conditions: Flat water on a protected tidal salt-marsh river

Current: Flood in/ebb out. Tide turns in area of Mill Pond 1 hour 15 minutes after launch.

Launch time: 2½ hours before Boston high

Permits, fees, parking: A town parking permit is required; however, you can offload your boat and then park your vehicle across Shore Road at the unpaved lot.

Facilities: None

Handicap access: Launch is off a rocky shore

Directions to launch: From the Bourne Bridge rotary, go 3.3 miles south on MA 28, then take a right onto Barlows Landing Road. Drive 1.7 miles to an intersection and turn right onto Shore Road. Go ¼ mile to bridge. Park in the dirt lot on the right after crossing the bridge. The launch area is across the road from the road.

The Tour

There are several reasons why you would want to paddle the Pocasset River: the wind in Phinneys Harbor is up and the Back River trip is impossible; hardly anyone paddles the Pocasset and you are in need of a quiet refuge; or you are a tourist with a notebook full of things to do and places to go with only a few hours to spare.

The Pocasset River was named for the Pocasset Iron Company, which had a mill on the river in the 1800s. Today it is a quiet area but for a small boatyard and a scattering of boat moorings at its mouth. In 1980, the Pocasset River Estuary was designated an area of critical environmental concern by the Massachusetts Department of Environmental Protection. It is hoped that what is learned here through research and study can be beneficially applied to other salt marshes.

Because this is a very leisurely paddle you will have the time to visit with many salt-marsh critters that otherwise go unnoticed. Begin your

*A great egret in search of breakfast in
the shallows of the Pocasset.*

trip by launching into the current and allowing it to carry you upstream. Carefully listen and look, and you may encounter mating blue crabs, predatory mantis shrimp, scavenging clam worms, or fiesty hermit crabs in constant search of bigger and better homes.

You may want to pack not only your binoculars but also a hand lens and a dip net. Use the net to sweep under the bladder wrack and catch shore shrimp, spider crabs, mummichogs, and periwinkles. Pick up an underwater stone and with your hand lens look for hydroids, anemones, and clusters of organ pipe sponge. This is just a small sample of the fascinating creatures you might find. Overall, the yearly biomass (both flora and fauna) produced by a salt marsh adds up to nearly 10 tons of organic matter per acre, almost 6 times more than that of a wheat field.

This healthy salt marsh offers a host of plants and animals in a peaceful sanctuary. Enjoy the serenity, and when the tide turns, paddle back to the launch site.

4.   Bassetts Island, Pocasset (Town of Bourne)

Maps:
> USGS Onset Quadrangle
> USGS Pocasset Quadrangle

Launch location: Town landing at the end of Barlows Landing Road

Habitats: Bay, coves, cedar- and pine-covered island

Length of trip: 3½ hours

Type of trip: Round-trip paddle with walk on the island

Paddling distance: 4½ miles; 8½ miles if you also paddle the shoreline of Red Brook Harbor and Hens Cove

Paddling conditions: Open bays

Current: Ebb out/flood in. Tide turns at the western point of Bassetts Island 1 hour after launch.

Launch time: On low, 2½ hours before Boston low

Permits, fees, parking: Town of Bourne permit sticker required for seasonal parking. No launch fees. If you do not have a town sticker, you can request permission to park at the church, or the restaurant located at the intersection of Barlows Landing Road and Shore Road.

Facilities: No facilities. Coffee shop and service station nearby.

Handicap access: Paved ramp

Directions to launch: From the Bourne Bridge rotary, go 3.3 miles south on MA 28, then turn right onto Barlows Landing Road. Drive 1.7 miles to the intersection of Barlows Landing Road and Shore Road, and continue on Barlows Landing Road (bearing left) to its end, where you can park and put in.

The Tour

Bassetts Island is flanked by Pocasset Harbor to the north and Red Brook Harbor to the southeast. The island was named in the 1700s after Colonel William Bassett, a selectman of Sandwich. It is a relatively narrow, small, three-cornered island. The southern end, approximately one-third of the island, is owned by the town of Bourne and open to the public. The remaining land is private, with a few houses inconspicuously located on the northern side. Once launched from the town landing at the end of Barlows Landing Road, it is a straight shot out to

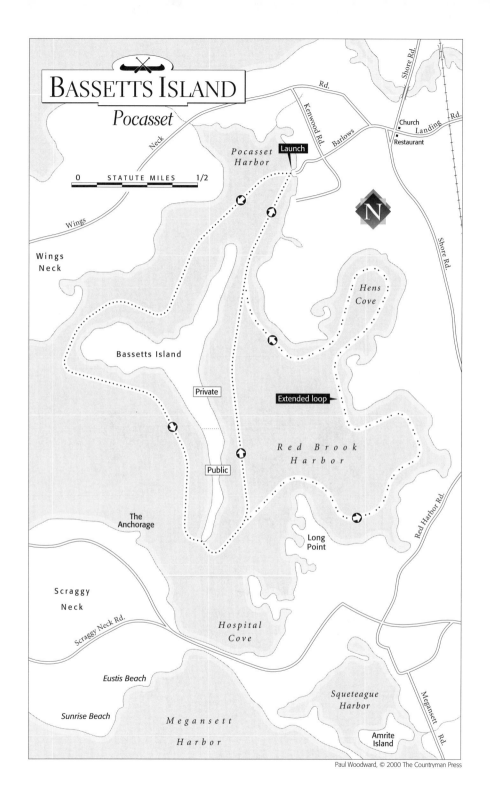

BASSETTS ISLAND
Pocasset

0   STATUTE MILES   1/2

Neck

Wings

Wings Neck

Pocasset Harbor

Launch

Hens Cove

Bassetts Island

Private

Extended loop

Red Brook Harbor

Public

The Anchorage

Long Point

Scraggy Neck

Scraggy Neck Rd.

Hospital Cove

Eustis Beach

Sunrise Beach

Megansett Harbor

Squeteague Harbor

Amrite Island

Kenwood Rd.

Rd.

Barlows

Church Landing   Rd.

Restaurant

Shore Rd.

Shore Rd.

Red Harbor Rd.

Megansett Rd.

N

Paul Woodward, © 2000 The Countryman Press

Canada geese frequent bays and rivers on the Cape,
but feed in the open grasslands along the shore.

the northern tip of the island. A paddle around the island makes for an easy round trip of 4½ miles.

On the Pocasset Harbor side of the island the shoreline is colonized by eastern red cedars. The gnarled shapes of the driftwood from these trees litter the shore, creating a collector's paradise. (This side of the island is private land, so obey the NO TRESPASSING signs.)

The public, or southern, end of the island is a wonderful place to beachcomb, and its inaccessibility makes it an inviting spot to picnic, swim, or sunbathe in relative privacy. At low tide, you can walk out on the sandflats to the boat channel. If you have a shellfish license (see the Resource Appendix), dig for your dinner. Plan a late afternoon trip and stay for a spectacular sunset over Buzzards Bay, accompanied by a parade of sailboats heading home with masts silhouetted by the setting sun.

Leaving the southern tip of Bassetts Island, keep its shore to your left until you reach Pocasset Harbor and Barlows Landing.

If you wish to extend your tour by an additional 4 miles, paddle from the southern tip of Bassetts Island over to Long Point. From there, paddle along the shore of Red Brook Harbor and Hens Cove. In early spring, don't be surprised if a harbor seal pokes its head out of the water to check you out.

5. *Sandwich Harbor, Sandwich*

Maps:
> USGS Sandwich Quadrangle

Launch location: Boardwalk Road, Sandwich

Habitats: Salt marsh and tidal creek

Length of trip:
> Mill Creek, 2 hours
> Springhill Creek, 4 hours

Type of trip: Round-trip paddle with walk on the marsh

Paddling distances:
> Mill Creek, 1½ miles
> Springhill Creek, 4 miles

Paddling conditions: Flatwater tidal creeks

Current: Flood in/ebb out. The tide turns in Mill Creek 1 hour after launch.

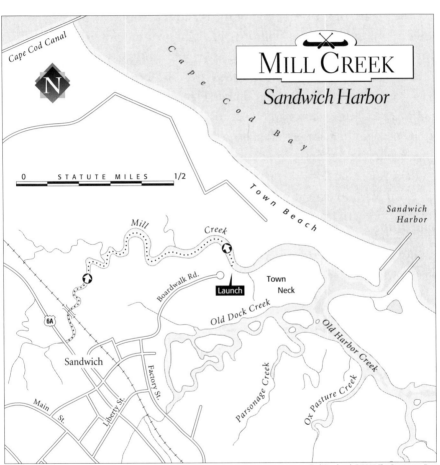

MILL CREEK

Sandwich Harbor

Cape Cod Canal

N

Cape Cod Bay

Town Beach

Sandwich Harbor

STATUTE MILES

0   1/2

Mill   Creek

Boardwalk Rd.

Launch

Town Neck

Old Dock Creek

6A

Sandwich

Factory St.

Liberty St.

Main St.

Parsonage Creek

Old Harbor Creek

Ox Pasture Creek

Paul Woodward, © 2000 The Countryman Press

In Springhill Creek, the tide turns in Springhill Marsh 2 hours
15 minutes after launch.

Launch times:
Mill Creek: On high, same as Boston high
Springhill Creek: On high, 45 minutes before Boston high.
(Paddle against the current for the first and last ½ mile.)

Permits, fees, parking: Small lot at Boardwalk Road, town stickers
required

Facilities: No facilities

Handicap access: No paved ramp, launch from beach to the right
of the boardwalk.

Directions to launch: Take exit 2 off US 6, and turn onto MA 130
north. After 1.2 miles, turn right onto School Street. In a very
short distance turn right onto Main Street, then left onto Liberty
Street. Cross MA 6A, then turn left onto Factory Street. In 0.1
mile, turn right onto Boardwalk Road, and follow it for 0.3 mile
to the parking lot.

The Tours

Mill Creek and Old Harbor Creek are the two major sources for water
that flows into Sandwich Harbor, and out into Cape Cod Bay. There are
a number of little feeder creeks, with interesting names such as Factory,
Old Dock, Parsonage, and Ox Pasture, that provide us with a glimpse
into the rich, historic past of the oldest town on Cape Cod. The town
of Sandwich was established in 1637 and by the 19th century was a
lively hub with two glass factories, in addition to one for tack and several for shoes.

Mill Creek

Mill Creek is a good choice if you are looking for a short, easy paddle.
Launch your boat alongside the boardwalk at the end of Boardwalk
Road. Paddle under the walkway and let the brisk current carry you
through the marsh. It was in this area, Town Neck, that the first settlers built their homes, pastured their cattle, and raised their families
back in the 1630s. Unfortunately, after only ¾ of a mile you will have
to stop, for MA 6A prevents you from going any farther. However, this

Periwinkles have a smooth shell and are slightly smaller than dog whelks, another common snail species.

is a good place to get out of your boat and explore the salt marsh on foot. Try bouncing up and down and feel the peat quiver like gelatin under you. Before getting back in your boat, gather up some periwinkles to take home with you to serve up a dish of *escargots à la Bourginonne,* that is, snails simmered in wine and served piping hot with garlic butter.

Caution: Don't confuse the browsing, vegetarian periwinkle, *Littorina littorea,* with the scavenging, omnivorous mud dog whelk, *Nassarius obsoletus.* Dog whelks are larger and tend to have rougher shells than periwinkles.

After collecting your periwinkles, watch for the turning tide and paddle or drift back to the launch at the boardwalk.

Old Harbor Creek and Environs

The first ½ mile of this round-trip paddle requires paddling against a stiff incoming current. Launch alongside the boardwalk, and you will be up against the tide until you reach Old Harbor Creek. The effort, however, is worth it. When you reach Old Harbor Creek the current is

The Sandwich Boardwalk is a prominent landmark on Mill Creek.

with you, and you can float into any one of the four creeks that branch off this main stem. The farthest creek is Springhill, so named for the numerous freshwater springs that feed it. Pine Island Creek features an island of upland plants and trees growing in the middle of a salt marsh. The area around Ox Pasture Creek, as the name implies, was ideal for pasturing cattle because of its accessibility and rich salt-marsh hay. Parsonage Creek got its name from the old tradition whereby farm- and pastureland was given to the church parson as payment for his services.

Whichever creek you take, the birding in the spring and fall is excellent. During the summer, paddle one of the winding creeks to the end and enjoy its beauty. You will know you have reached the end when you see the railroad tracks, or hear the whistle of the Cape Cod Scenic Railroad as it journeys along the marsh from Sandwich to Barnstable.

The cordgrass and salt-marsh hay that cover the area become rivulets of flowing grass as the tide turns, telling you it is time to make

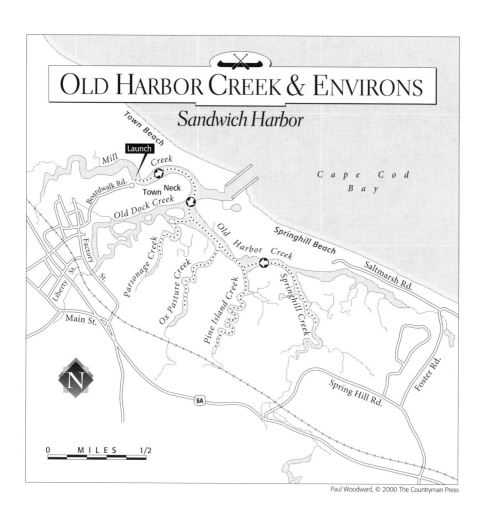

OLD HARBOR CREEK & ENVIRONS

Sandwich Harbor

Town Beach

Launch

Mill

Creek

Boardwalk Rd.

Town Neck

Old Dock Creek

Cape Cod
Bay

Springhill Beach

Saltmarsh Rd.

Old Harbor Creek

Parsonage Creek

Ox Pasture Creek

Pine Island Creek

Springhill Creek

Factory St.

Liberty St.

Main St.

Spring Hill Rd.

Foster Rd.

6A

N

0   MILES   1/2

your way back. Before attempting the ½-mile paddle against the current in Mill Creek, stop for a rest at the beach along Old Harbor Creek. Once you reach Mill Creek and feel the current against you, maintain a steady, even pace and don't slack off; you will make progress if you keep paddling. No time to rest, or you will have to recover lost ground or be swept out into Cape Cod Bay!

6. *Scorton Creek, East Sandwich*

Maps:
> USGS Sandwich Quadrangle

Launch location: State Wildlife Reservation, East Sandwich

Habitats: Salt marsh, tidal creeks

Length of trip: 3 hours; 4 hours with optional one-way to East Sandwich Beach

Type of trip: Round-trip paddle with a walk on Talbots Point. An optional one-way paddle is possible if a car is spotted at East Sandwich Beach.

Paddling distance: 2½ miles

Paddling conditions: Well-protected flat water on creeks

Current: Flood in/ebb out. Tide turns at Shove Creek Marsh 2 hours 15 minutes after launch.

Launch time: On high, 1 hour before Boston high.

Permits, fees, parking: No parking stickers required at State Wildlife Reservation area, which has a small, unpaved dirt parking lot. Parking at East Sandwich Beach is available for a few vehicles at the corner of Ploughed Neck Road and North Shore Road; permits are not required.

Facilities: No facilities on-site, service station and convenience store nearby

Handicap access: At the State Wildlife Reservation area you are required to launch from a salt-marsh bank. East Sandwich Beach is vehicle accessible only at low tide by driving and parking on sandflats at the end of Holway Road.

Directions to launch: From US 6, take exit 3, and follow Quaker Meeting House Road north to MA 6A east. Turn right onto MA 6A and continue 1.5 miles. Just before the Scorton Creek Bridge, turn right onto a gravel road, and go 0.2 mile to a parking lot.

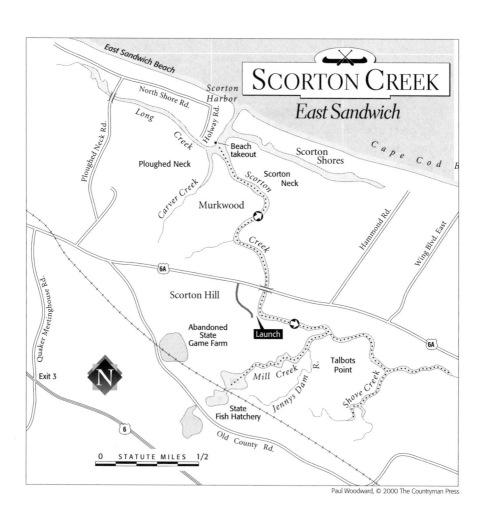

SCORTON CREEK

East Sandwich

East Sandwich Beach

North Shore Rd.

Scorton Harbor

Holway Rd.

Long Creek

Ploughed Neck Rd.

Ploughed Neck

Carver Creek

Murkwood

Beach takeout

Scorton

Scorton Neck

Scorton Shores

Cape Cod B

Hammond Rd.

Wing Blvd. East

Creek

6A

Scorton Hill

Quaker Meetinghouse Rd.

Exit 3

Abandoned State Game Farm

Launch

6A

N

Mill Creek

Jennys Dam R.

Talbots Point

Shove Creek

State Fish Hatchery

6

Old County Rd.

0   STATUTE MILES   1/2

For East Sandwich Beach, take exit 3 off US 6 as above, following Quaker Meeting House Road to MA 6A. Turn right onto MA 6A, and drive 0.8 mile. Turn left onto Ploughed Neck Road, go 0.8 mile, and turn right onto North Shore Road. After 0.4 mile, turn right onto Holway Road.

The Tour

Scorton Creek is "the place where the stream branches." Its name is thought to derive from the Algonquian Indian word *scautun*. The creek branches north to Scorton Harbor and east to the Great Marsh, with Barnstable Harbor beyond. Before the 1800s it would have been possible to paddle from Scorton Harbor to Barnstable Harbor, but today roads and houses impede this passage.

Scorton Creek is tidal. If you put in at the State Wildlife Reservation on an incoming tide, you will have ample time and sufficient water to explore the salt marsh. The first sizable creek off Scorton Creek is Mill. Following Mill Creek to Jennys Dam River will bring you to Talbots Point Salt Marsh Wildlife Reservation. Take time for a short hike along the trail that overlooks the marsh. You can almost see the farmers of the 17th, 18th, and 19th centuries standing on the marsh and cutting

Boaters pull ashore for a beach-combing leg stretch.

EVENDEN
'99

The great blue heron stalks its prey in shallow water.

salt-marsh hay. After the hay was cut it was piled onto wooden frames, called "staddles," to dry. You can still find the bases of these staddles if you look for them on the marsh.

Return to Scorton Creek and paddle into the next good-sized branch, Shove Creek, perhaps named for the "pushing and shoving" required to get a boat through as the creek narrows inland. Birds can be found in the salt marsh during any season, but spring migration is the time of the most activity. The red-winged blackbird is a sure sign that spring has arrived. Listen for their distinct *kon-ke-re* as they descend in flocks upon the marsh, proclaiming their breeding territory. Throughout the summer months, great blue herons quietly stalk the tidal creeks in search of fish and eels. Overhead, common and least terns dive for mummichogs. Other summer birds found in the marsh include green-backed herons, snowy egrets, and tree and barn swallows, busily catching insects on the wing. As you wind your way along the creek, look out over the marsh, and you may spot a northern harrier in search of meadow vole. You will pass under the nesting platform of a pair of osprey who have nested here for eight years.

Explore the creeks, but do keep an eye on the tide. When it turns it will drop about 6 inches every 15 minutes, and if you don't go out with the flow, you may find yourself aground and waiting for the next flood tide (about 6 hours). Paddle with the ebb tide until you reach the launch site. You can take out here or continue on to East Sandwich Beach. (Spot a vehicle here if you plan to finish your trip here. Otherwise you will have to paddle 1½ miles back against the tide.) After passing under MA 6A, the creek will widen and meander for another 1½ miles. The water becomes a crystal clear emerald green, allowing you to search the peat banks for crabs and snails as you slowly drift by. Striped bass are also easy to spot in the water around murkwood.

The takeout is on the beach to your left, past Long Creek, and before the channel opening into the bay. *Caution:* The current is very swift through the channel as the water pours into Cape Cod Bay.

7. *Washburn Island, Falmouth*

Maps:
> USGS Falmouth Quadrangle
> USGS Cotuit Quadrangle

Launch location: Great River Boat Landing, Mashpee
Habitats: Open bay, island, tidal pond, barrier beach
Length of trip: 4 hours
Type of trip: Round-trip paddle and walk on Washburn Island
Paddling distance: 4 miles
Paddling conditions: Open bay
Current: Ebb out/flood in. Tide turns at Dead Neck 2 hours 45 minutes after launch.
Launch time: On low, 2 hours before Boston low
Permits, fees, parking: No permits or fees required to park or launch. Great River Boat Landing has a medium-sized, paved lot.
Facilities: None. Campsites on Washburn Island provide an option for longer stays.

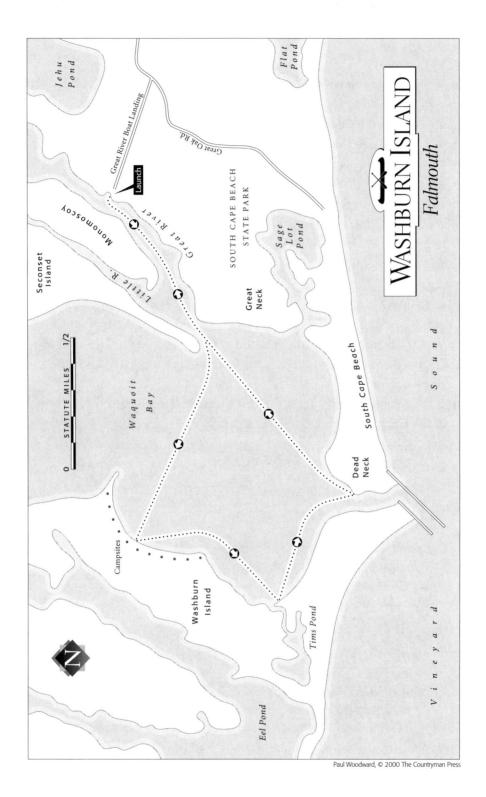

WASHBURN ISLAND

Falmouth

Jehu Pond

Flat Pond

Great River Boat Landing

Great Oak Rd.

Launch

Great River

Monomoscoy

Little R.

Seconset Island

SOUTH CAPE BEACH STATE PARK

Great Neck

Sage Lot Pond

Waquoit Bay

STATUTE MILES

0   1/2

South Cape Beach

Dead Neck

Sound

Campsites

Washburn Island

Tims Pond

Vineyard

Eel Pond

N

Paul Woodward, © 2000 The Countryman Press

Handicap access: Paved ramp

Directions to launch: Take exit 5 off US 6, then turn onto MA 149 south. At its intersection with MA 28, turn right and go approximately 5 miles until you come to the Mashpee rotary. Exit off the rotary onto Great Neck Road South (you'll see a sign for New Seabury). Go 2.7 miles; bear left onto Great Oak Road. After drive 1.9 miles look for the green sign for Great River Boat Landing; turn right and follow the road 0.6 mile to the landing.

The Tour

Paddle down Great River into Waquoit Bay. At the mouth of the river, paddle west, across the bay, to Washburn Island (watch for boat traffic in the channel). Except for the boat channel into Vineward Sound, the water is only 4 to 5 feet deep. As you approach Washburn, the full beauty of this 330-acre island comes into view. It is a testament to grassroots organizations and the dedication of local folks that this island is preserved. What was slated to become Wind Echo Island development, with 50 luxury homes, a dock, and yacht club, was taken by right of eminent domain by the Commonwealth in 1981 and remains in its natural state for all of us to enjoy.

Make a stop on this pine-barren island, and walk the remains of roads built in the early 1940s when Washburn Island was a training site for the U.S. Army's Amphibious Corps. Imagine what it was like back then! Now you can find repose in a diverse habitat of pine and oak forests, saltwater ponds, and barrier beaches.

Back on the water, paddle south past the campground. There are 11 primitive campsites on Washburn Island managed by the Massachusetts State Park Service. Reservations may be made by calling 877-422-6762. There is neither running water nor public facilities.

Stop at Tim's Pond for a look at a coastal saltwater pond. This body of water serves as home to a pair of osprey who have been returning to this nest for a number of years. The size of the nest reveals many seasons of replenishment. With binoculars you can view an array of little birds darting into and out of the nest, feeding on insects and thereby helping to keep the nest clean for the adult osprey and their chicks.

For the return trip, paddle along the barrier beach, across the boat channel, and stop for a break at Dead Neck. Take a walk to the rocks that line the channel for a perfect view of Vineyard Sound and in the distance, Martha's Vineyard. Launching again, keep the shore on your right until you enter the Great River. At the fork, bear right, and continue up Great River to the landing.

8.　*South Cape Beach, Mashpee*

Maps:
　　USGS Falmouth Quadrangle
　　USGS Cotuit Quadrangle
Launch location: Great River Landing, Mashpee
Habitats: Tidal river, bay, barrier beach
Length of trip: 3 hours
Type of trip: Round-trip paddle and walk on South Cape Beach
Paddling distance: 4 miles
Paddling conditions: Open bay
Current: Ebb out/flood in. Tide turns at Dead Neck 1 hour 30 minutes after launch.
Launch time: On low, 45 minutes before Boston low
Permits, fees, parking: No permits or fees required to park or launch. Great River Landing has a medium-sized, paved lot.
Facilities: None
Handicap access: Paved ramp
Directions to launch: Take exit 5 off US 6, then turn onto MA 149 south. At its intersection with MA 28, turn right and go approximately 5 miles until you come to the Mashpee rotary. Exit off the rotary onto Great Neck Road South (you'll see a sign for New Seabury). Go 2.7 miles, bear left onto Great Oak Road, then drive 1.9 miles and, after the green sign for Great River Boat Landing, turn right and follow the road 0.6 mile to the landing.

The Tour

A launch on an outgoing tide from the town landing on Great River Landing Road will begin your paddle down the Great River, a glacial outwash channel. The river is very narrow until you reach the end of

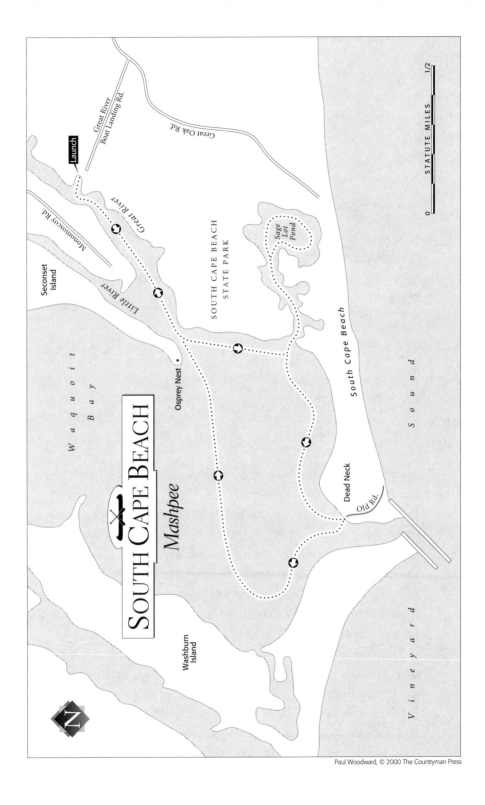

SOUTH CAPE BEACH

Mashpee

Launch

Great River
Boat Landing Rd.

Great Oak Rd.

Great River

Monomoscoy Rd.

Little River

Seconset
Island

Osprey Nest

SOUTH CAPE BEACH
STATE PARK

Sage
Lot
Pond

South Cape Beach

Sound

Dead Neck

Old Rd.

Waquoit Bay

Washburn
Island

Vineyard

N

0   1/2

STATUTE MILES

Paul Woodward, © 2000 The Countryman Press

Great egrets, looking out over South Cape Beach.

Monomoscoy Peninsula, where it merges with the Little River. There is a fair amount of powerboat traffic at this point due to a boatyard on the Little River; if you stay to the left of the channel markers, you can avoid these boats and still have enough water to navigate over the sandbar into Waquoit Bay. Don't miss the large osprey nest on the platform to your right as you leave the river. It has been an active nest for a number of years and will continue to be so as long as nothing happens to the breeding pair. Ospreys mate for life, and these two fish hawks have successfully fledged many young over the years.

Once into the bay, head south (the shore will be on your left) for ½ mile. On your left you will see the entrance to Sage Lot Pond, a coastal salt pond. If the water is deep enough, paddle in. At low tide this is an excellent spot to see a variety of shorebirds such as willets, yellow legs, and both semipalmated and piping plovers. On the marsh you may see great blue herons and great egrets. Watch the tide as well as the birds; if you spend too much time in Sage Lot, you will have to "frog" (pull or carry your boat over sandbars) your way out.

Leaving Sage Lot, paddle west to Dead Neck, the place where South Cape Beach and Washburn Island meet at the boat channel into Vineyard Sound. Take out on the South Cape Beach side and take a stroll along the shore to observe the dynamics of wave action and longshore drift, or just beachcomb for shells and whelk egg cases. In spring, you may see wire enclosures along the upper beach that are used to protect nesting piping plovers. The Waquoit Bay National Estuarine Reserve has an avid and active group of volunteers who monitor the shoreline in search of nesting piping plovers. Plovers lay their eggs directly on the sand in the middle of the beach, where they are vulnerable to predators and human traffic. Once a nest is identified, a wire enclosure is placed around it to keep predators away. These birds are listed as threatened by both the state of Massachusetts and the United States.

Return to your boat by walking the old road that runs down the middle of this barrier beach. Look for savannah and fox sparrows in among the salt spray rose and American beach grass that grow on the dunes. Be wary of poison ivy, which spreads its vines along the sand, but do enjoy munching on a beach pea when in season.

On the return paddle across the boat channel, keep the shore to your left and stop to watch commercial clammers working their grants. Visit, but do not disturb, for they only have a few hours between tides to make a living.

Now, point your bow northeast and begin the 1-mile paddle across the bay. Try to spot the osprey nest on the point of Seconset Island at the entrance into Great River. Once into the river, keep the shore on your right until you reach the landing.

9. *Waquoit Bay's Tidal Rivers and Salt Ponds, Falmouth*

Maps:
USGS Falmouth Quadrangle
USGS Cotuit Quadrangle

Launch locations:
>Moonakis River, Great River Landing, Mashpee
>Jehu and Hamblin Salt Ponds, Great River Landing, Mashpee
>Childs River/Waquoit Bay, Whites Landing Road, Falmouth

Habitats: Tidal rivers, bay, woodland, bogs, brackish marsh

Length of trips:
>Moonakis River, 4 hours
>Jehu and Hamblin Salt Ponds, 4 hours
>Childs River/Waquoit Bay, 5 hours

Type of trip: Round-trip paddle and walk

Paddling distances:
>Moonakis River, 6½ miles
>Jehu and Hamblin Salt Ponds, 7½ miles
>Childs River/Waquoit Bay, 9 miles

Paddling conditions: Tidal rivers, open bay

Current:
>Moonakis River, flood in/ebb out. Tide turns at Town
>   Conservaton Lands 2 hours 30 minutes after launch.
>Jehu and Hamblin Salt Ponds, flood in/ebb out. Tide turns in
>   Jehu Pond 2 hours 15 minutes after launch.
>Childs River/Waquoit Bay, ebb out/flood in. Tide turns at Dead
>   Neck 3 hours 45 minutes after launch.

Launch times:
>Moonakis River, on high, 1 hour before Boston high
>Jehu and Hamblin Salt Ponds, on high, 45 minutes before
>   Boston high
>Childs River/Waquoit Bay, on low, 3 hours
>   before Boston low

Permits, fees, parking: No permits or fees required to park or
launch. Great River Landing has a medium-sized, paved lot.
Whites Landing Road has a large, unpaved lot approximately
300 feet from the ramp.

Facilities: None

Handicap access: Paved ramp at both locations

Directions to launch: Great River Landing: Take exit 5 off US 6, then
turn onto MA 149 south. At its intersection with MA 28, turn right
and go approximately 5 miles until you come to the Mashpee
rotary. Exit off the rotary onto Great Neck Road South (you'll see
a sign for New Seabury). After 2.7 miles bear left onto Great Oak

Fiddler crabs can be seen feeding in huge numbers at low tide.

Road, then drive 1.9 miles and, after the green sign for Great River Boat Landing, turn right and follow the road 0.6 mile to the landing.

Whites Landing Road: From the Mashpee rotary take MA 28 North toward Falmouth. Go 3 miles, cross the bridge, and immediately after passing Edwards Boatyard turn left onto Whites Landing Road.

The Tours

Waquoit Bay is located within the towns of Falmouth and Mashpee on the southern shore of Cape Cod. It is protected from the waters of Vineyard Sound by the barrier beaches of South Cape Beach and Washburn Island and managed by the Waquoit Bay National Estuarine Research Reserve (WBNERR). The bay is shallow, approximately 2 miles long and 1 mile wide. It is bounded to the west by the pristine and undeveloped 330-acre Washburn Island, and to the south by the 500-acre South Cape Beach State Park. To the east are the Moonakis, Little, and Great Rivers; and Hamblin, Jehu, and Sage Lot Ponds. The 2,500-acre reserve offers a multitude of habitats with numerous rivers and salt ponds to paddle. We will detail a number of paddling routes in the Waquoit Bay system, but it is just a beginning, and we encourage you to explore others on your own.

Moonakis River

You will need to launch from Great River Landing on an incoming tide in order to have sufficient water for this trip on the Moonakis River. After you launch, on a southwest tack, you will be against the tide until you enter Waquoit Bay. Paddling against the tide here is not very difficult as long as you don't have a stiff wind against you. Once you enter the bay, swing north along the eastern shore and let the predominant southwest wind guide you to the entrance of the Moonakis.

The bay's largest source of fresh water originates in Johns Pond (about 2 miles north); from there it flows down the Quashnet and into the brackish Moonakis, traversing forests, cranberry bogs, residential areas, and golf courses along the way.

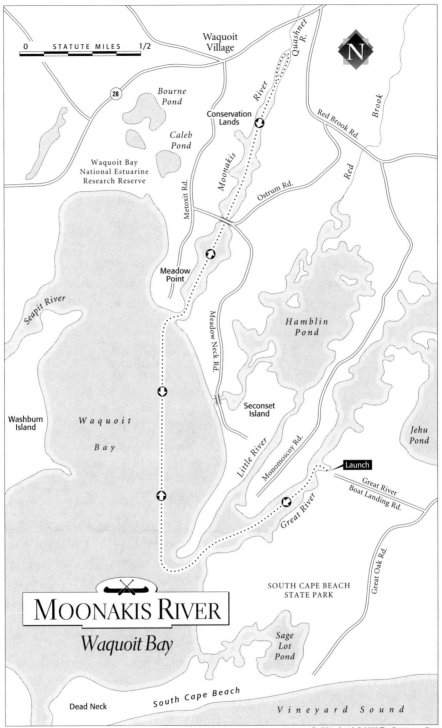

STATUTE MILES

0   1/2

Waquoit
Village

Quashnet R.

N

*Bourne
Pond*

28

Conservation
Lands

Red Brook Rd.

Brook

*Caleb
Pond*

Waquoit Bay
National Estuarine
Research Reserve

Moonakis River

Ostrum Rd.

Red

Metoxit Rd.

Seapit River

Meadow
Point

Meadow Neck Rd.

*Hamblin
Pond*

Washburn
Island

Waquoit

Bay

Seconset
Island

*Jehu
Pond*

Little River

Monomoscoy Rd.

Launch

Great River

Great River
Boat Landing Rd.

Great River

Great Oak Rd.

SOUTH CAPE BEACH
STATE PARK

MOONAKIS RIVER

Waquoit Bay

*Sage
Lot
Pond*

Dead Neck

South Cape Beach

Vineyard Sound

Paul Woodward, © 2000 The Countryman Press

Enter the Moonakis from Waquoit Bay by way of the salt-marsh creek and then head upriver for a rest stop at conservation lands owned by the town of Falmouth, on the west side of the river. The site is marked by a picnic table. Take a walk through the woods atop the dikes of this abandoned cranberry bog. Before the tide turns, make your way to the upper reaches of the Moonakis, where the water turns fresh and you can paddle no farther. A journey on foot would be the best way to reach the Quashnet River, and only bushwhackers would attempt to navigate the Quashnet—it is completely overgrown with vegetation. The river is a catch-and-release area for sea-run brook trout as well as part of the 500-acre Quashnet River Corridor. Bordered by uplands and abandoned cranberry bogs, the river and its protected corridor are managed by the Waquoit Bay National Estuarine Research Reserve. Before you retreat with the outgoing tide, glance back at the vegetated Quashnet and recognize that such a small stream, together with groundwater seepage and precipitation, plays an important part in maintaining the balance of this estuarine ecosystem.

Jehu and Hamblin Ponds

Launch from Great River Landing, go right, and paddle into Jehu Pond. The Great River, which flows in and out of Jehu Pond, is supplied with fresh water from Abigail's Brook. Both Hamblin and Jehu Ponds have houses along their shores; however, Jehu Pond is less developed because it is part of the Mashpee National Wildlife Refuge System (MNWRS). The MNWRS contains 362 acres of salt marsh, uplands, and abandoned cranberry bogs. Make a stop here and hike the trails. There is a great trail through a cedar swamp and out to the marsh. This is an excellent habitat for bird-watching.

When the tide turns, paddle downriver, swing around the southern point of Monomoscoy Peninsula, and paddle up into the Little River. The Little River is a tidal river that flows into and out of Hamblin Pond, which is supplied with a small amount of fresh water from Red Brook. You will be working against the tide on the way in to this saltwater pond, bordered to the north by a small salt marsh with an active osprey nest. This is a good spot to pause and watch these skillful fish hawks dive for

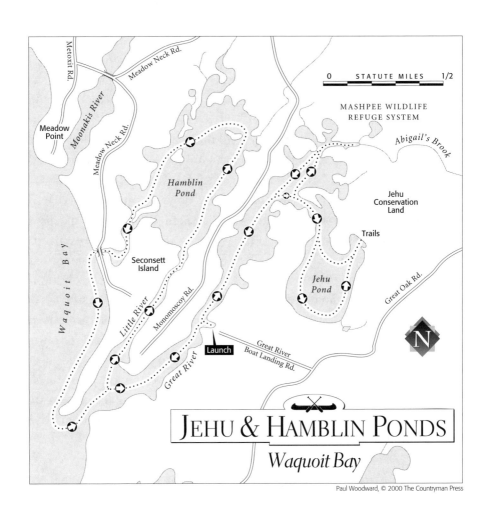

Metoxit Rd.

Meadow Neck Rd.

0 STATUTE MILES 1/2

MASHPEE WILDLIFE
REFUGE SYSTEM

Moonakis River

Abigail's Brook

Meadow
Point

Meadow Neck Rd.

Hamblin
Pond

Jehu
Conservation
Land

Trails

Seconsett
Island

Little River

Monomoscoy Rd.

Jehu
Pond

Great Oak Rd.

Waquoit Bay

Launch

Great River

Great River
Boat Landing Rd.

N

JEHU & HAMBLIN PONDS

Waquoit Bay

Paul Woodward, © 2000 The Countryman Press

their prey from high overhead. After exploring Hamblin Pond, exit the pond to the southwest by passing through the culvert that enters into Waquoit Bay. Keep the shore to your left and paddle around the southern tip of Seconset Island and back to the launch at Great River Landing.

Childs River/Waquoit Bay

The Childs River, which, like the Moonakis, originates in Johns Pond, is Waquoit Bay's second largest source of fresh water. There is a town landing on the river with a large public parking area. This is a very popular launch location in summer. The river here is strictly tidal, but a short paddle north will take you beyond the boat traffic and into brackish water, where you might happen upon some dabbling ducks, tails pointing skyward as they submerge their heads to feed on vegetation.

For a loop trip of Waquoit Bay, head downriver until you see Washburn Island on your left. Turn into the Seapit River, keeping the mainland shore to your left and the island to your right. As you paddle through, you will pass shellfish grants, and you will emerge into Waquoit Bay. The former Swift Estate, now the Waquoit Bay National Estuarine Research Reserve's (WBNERR) headquarters, is situated on a hill to the north overlooking the bay. Stop and take a tour to learn what WBNERR is doing to preserve and protect this valuable resource. Back on the water, circle the bay, paddling south to Dead Neck. Take a rest break; the tide should now be coming in. Complete your journey back to the Child's River Landing by paddling along the eastern and northern shores of Washburn Island, turning left into the Seapit River and then right up into the Childs.

10. *Fullers Marsh, Cotuit (Town of Barnstable)*

Maps:
  USGS Cotuit Quadrangle
Launch location: Pirates Cove Town Landing, Mashpee Neck Road, Mashpee
Habitats: Bay, salt marsh, pine and oak forest

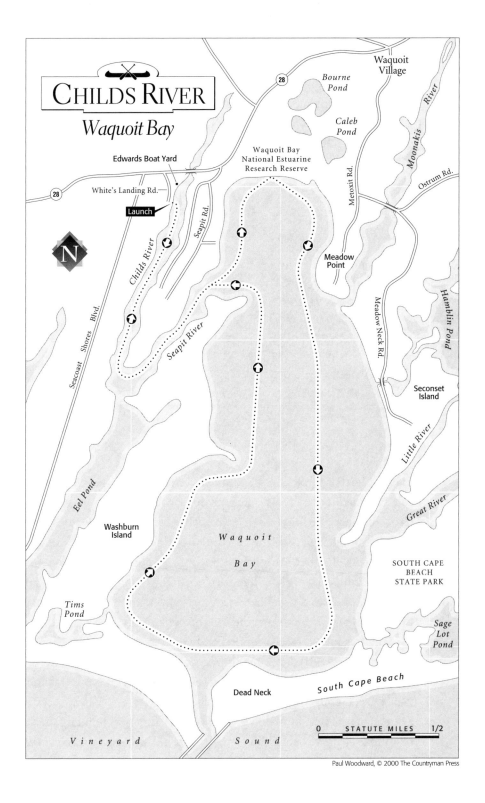

CHILDS RIVER

Waquoit Bay

Edwards Boat Yard

White's Landing Rd.

Launch

28

N

Childs River

Seapit Rd.

Seacoast Shores Blvd.

Seapit River

Eel Pond

Washburn
Island

Tims
Pond

28

Bourne
Pond

Caleb
Pond

Waquoit
Village

Moonakis River

Waquoit Bay
National Estuarine
Research Reserve

Metoxit Rd.

Ostrum Rd.

Meadow
Point

Meadow Neck Rd.

Hamblin Pond

Seconset
Island

Little River

Great River

W a q u o i t

B a y

SOUTH CAPE
BEACH
STATE PARK

Sage
Lot
Pond

Dead Neck

South Cape Beach

0   STATUTE MILES   1/2

V i n e y a r d   *S o u n d*

Paul Woodward, © 2000 The Countryman Press

Length of trip: 2½ hours
Type of trip: Round-trip paddle with a walk on Crocker Neck
Paddling distance: 2½ miles
Paddling conditions: Open bay into protected cove and salt-marsh creek
Current: Flood in/ebb out. Tide turns in Fullers Marsh 1 hour 30 minutes after launch.
Launch time: On high, 15 minutes before Boston high
Permits, fees, parking: No parking permits or launching fees required. Small, paved lot and off-road parking permitted.
Facilities: No facilities
Handicap access: Paved ramp
Directions to launch: From US 6, take exit 5. Drive on MA 149 south for approximately 7 miles, and then turn right onto MA 28 north. Go 3.5 miles and turn left onto Orchard Road. Drive 0.5 mile and turn right onto Quinaquisset Avenue. A quick left will take you onto Mashpee Neck Road; it's 1.5 miles to the town landing.

The Tour

Fullers Marsh is located in the southwestern corner of the village of Cotuit. It is surrounded by a 97-acre, town-owned conservation area called Crocker Neck. Begin your paddle with a launch from Pirates Cove Town Landing. This is the mouth of Shoestring Bay, named for its long and narrow channel. Paddle east out into Popponesset Bay, keeping Ryefield Point on your left, then turn north into Pinquickset Cove. The name Pinquickset is probably an anglicized version of the Algonquian word *punukqueëkontu,* meaning "on the bank of the river."

There is much to see, explore, and enjoy in this sheltered, shallow cove. It is a lively spot to watch the sleek and graceful great blue herons and egrets stalk their prey. Keep your eyes peeled below your boat and watch green crabs dig in as you approach. This is a very healthy estuarine marsh. It provides food, shelter, and nesting sites to many species of animals, from the smallest shore shrimp, hiding below the rockweed, to the majestic osprey hovering above.

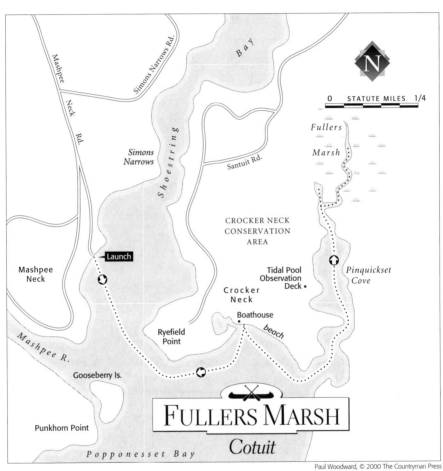

Mashpee Neck Rd.

Simons Narrows Rd.

Bay

Mashpee Neck Rd.

Shoestring

Simons Narrows

Santuit Rd.

Fullers Marsh

Launch

CROCKER NECK CONSERVATION AREA

Mashpee Neck

Tidal Pool Observation Deck •

Pinquickset Cove

Crocker Neck

Boathouse

beach

Ryefield Point

Mashpee R.

Gooseberry Is.

Punkhorn Point

FULLERS MARSH

Cotuit

Popponesset Bay

Paul Woodward, © 2000 The Countryman Press

STATUTE MILES
0   1/4

Paddle north, up into Fullers Marsh where the channel will fork left and right. Explore them both. Take the right channel and you will pass a manufactured platform with a nest occupied by a pair of osprey who have made this their summer home for many years. The channel begins to narrow as you approach the upland. The stream goes no farther than a dike built many years ago to prevent tidal flow so that the area could be converted into commercial cranberry bogs. The bogs have since been abandoned and are now invaded by common reed.

Crocker Neck Conservation Area is bounded by almost 2 miles of maintained walking trails. There are also picnic tables and lookout areas. After leaving Fullers Marsh and entering Popponesset Bay, on your right you will see a boathouse and beach where you can make a stop and explore the area.

11. *Santuit River, Cotuit (Town of Barnstable)*

Maps:
> USGS Cotuit Quadrangle

Launch location: Pirates Cove Town Landing, Mashpee Neck Road, Mashpee

Habitats: Bay, tidal river, salt marsh, brackish marsh

Length of trip: 3½ hours

Type of trip: Round-trip paddle

Paddling distance: 4½ miles

Paddling conditions: Open bay into protected tidal river

Current: Flood in/ebb out. Tide turns in the Santuit River 2 hours 30 minutes after launch.

Launch time: On high, 1 hour before Boston high

Permits, fees, parking: No permits or fees required. Small, paved lot. Off-road parking allowed.

Facilities: No facilities

Handicap access: Paved ramp

Directions to launch: From US 6, take exit 5. Drive on MA 149 south, and then turn right onto MA 28 north. Go 3.5 miles and turn left onto Orchard Road. Drive another 0.5 mile and turn right onto Quinaquisset Avenue. A quick left will take you onto Mashpee Neck Road; it's 1.5 miles to the town landing.

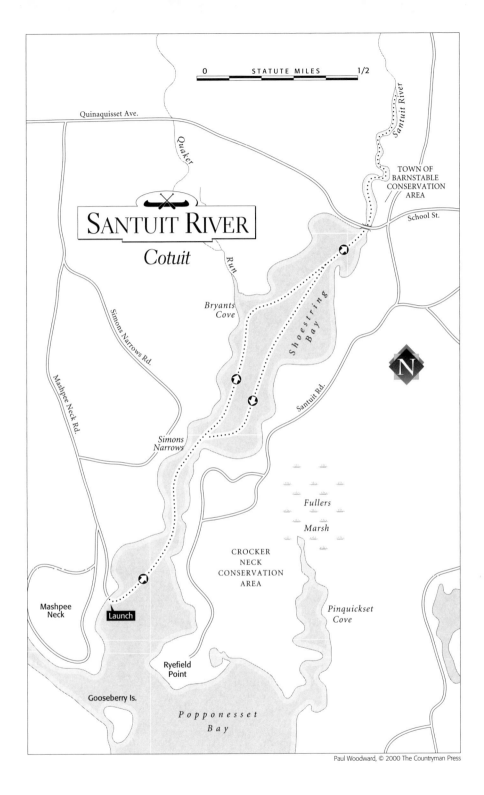

STATUTE MILES

0   1/2

Santuit River

Quinaquisset Ave.

Quaker

SANTUIT RIVER

Cotuit

Run

TOWN OF
BARNSTABLE
CONSERVATION
AREA

School St.

*Bryants
Cove*

*Shoestring
Bay*

Simons Narrows Rd.

Santuit Rd.

Mashpee Neck Rd.

*Simons
Narrows*

N

*Fullers

Marsh*

CROCKER
NECK
CONSERVATION
AREA

*Pinquickset
Cove*

Mashpee
Neck

Launch

Ryefield
Point

Gooseberry Is.

*Popponesset
Bay*

Paul Woodward, © 2000 The Countryman Press

EVENDEN '99

Estuary denizens include the muskrat and green heron.

The Tour

The Santuit River begins its journey to the sea at Santuit Pond. As it leaves the pond, it is but a small freshwater stream that wends its way south, obstructed by roads and housing developments. The fresh water merges with salt water coming in from Shoestring Bay (so named because it is long and narrow) on the rising tide. On the ebb, the now-mingled waters flow out into Shoestring Bay, then Popponesset Bay, eventually reaching Nantucket Sound.

The best launch location for paddling the saltwater portion of the river is from Pirates Cove Landing on Mashpee Neck Road. As you head up Shoestring Bay you will soon pass through Simons Narrows, after which the bay opens up. Still, it is only about ½ mile across at its widest, making it possible to take shelter from the prevailing southwesterlies. On the west side of the bay is a creek called Quaker Run. We recommend you make a trip up the creek to explore this little salt-marsh area. On the way out, to your left, is a public area where you can get out and take a walk up the bluff for a scenic overlook of the river. Back out on the bay, continue north to the School Street bridge. With an incoming tide, you can easily pass under the span and into the Santuit River. Here, the houses become fewer. The introduction of fresh water becomes evident as cattails and phragmites (common reed) appear. This brackish river marsh is an active feeding ground for osprey from above and muskrat from below. In summer the swamp roses bloom in profusion, making passage somewhat tenable. On the eastern shore is conservation land, where you can stop, stretch your legs, and prepare for the return journey when the tide has turned, allowing passage under the bridge.

12. *Popponesset Beach and Meadow Point, Mashpee and Cotuit*

Maps:
USGS Cotuit Quadrangle
Launch location: Ockway Bay Landing, Mashpee
Habitats: Bay, barrier beach
Length of trip: 3 hours
Type of trip: Round-trip paddle with walk on Popponesset Beach
Paddling distance: 4 miles
Paddling conditions: Open bay and protected channel
Current: Ebb out/flood in. Tide turns at Popponesset Beach 1 hour 45 minutes after launch.
Launch time: On low, same as Boston low
Permits, fees, parking: No permits or fees required to park or launch. Parking at medium-sized, dirt lot.
Facilities: Freshwater spigot, no other facilities
Handicap access: Steep, paved ramp
Directions to launch: From US 6, take exit 5. Turn onto MA 149 south until you come to MA 28. Turn right onto MA 28 and drive approximately 5 miles to the Mashpee rotary. Take Great Neck Road South, following the signs to New Seabury. Drive 2.5 miles to the Ockway Bay Landing parking lot on the left.

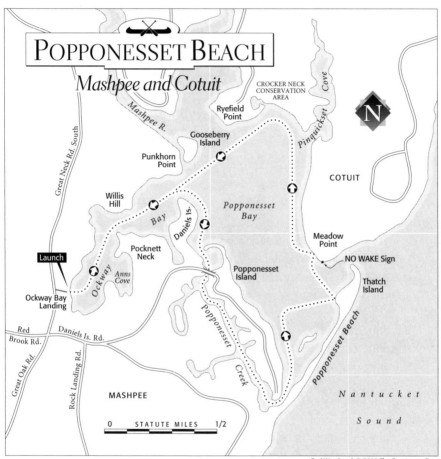

POPPONESSET BEACH

Mashpee and Cotuit

Mashpee R.

CROCKER NECK
CONSERVATION
AREA

Ryefield
Point

Pinquickset Cove

N

Gooseberry
Island

Great Neck Rd. South

Punkhorn
Point

COTUIT

Willis
Hill

*Popponesset
Bay*

Meadow
Point

Bay

Daniels Is.

NO WAKE Sign

Pocknett
Neck

Ockway

Popponesset
Island

Thatch
Island

Launch

Anns
Cove

Ockway Bay
Landing

Popponesset Creek

Popponesset Beach

Red
Brook Rd.

Daniels Is. Rd.

Great Oak Rd.

Rock Landing Rd.

N a n t u c k e t

MASHPEE

S o u n d

0   STATUTE MILES   1/2

Paul Woodward, © 2000 The Countryman Press

The Tour

This trip will take you along the entire shoreline of Popponesset Bay. Popponesset, from the Algonquian meaning "frost fish" or "winter tom cod," is one of many shallow embayments on the glacial outwash plain on the south side of Cape Cod.

Begin by paddling across Ockway Bay. On Pocknett Neck is an osprey nest on a platform along the eastern shore. The local electric company has erected many of these nesting platforms on poles throughout the Cape, and they have proven very successful in helping the osprey recover after DDT was banned in the 1960s.

Paddle into Popponesset Bay, keeping the shore to your right, and enter the inlet where you will see a few boats at anchor. Up ahead is a bridge that connects Popponesset Island with the mainland. The community of grandiose summer homes, known as New Seabury, has replaced the modest summer cottages of bygone days. After paddling under the bridge into Popponesset Creek, don't be surprised if you get the feeling that somehow you have ended up in one of coastal Florida's canals. After passing through Popponesset Creek, head for Thatch Island. Stop here and take a walk along the beach for views of Nantucket Sound. You may find the end of Popponesset Beach roped off, protecting the nests of the state and federally listed threatened piping plover. The birds themselves are hard to spot, for their sandy color provides excellent camouflage.

From Thatch Island, head north across the boat channel to Meadow Point in Cotuit. Meadow Point is conservation land and has been acquired by the Barnstable Land Trust. However, the house on the point is private property. Take out where you see the NO WAKE sign and walk along the shore to the marsh and tidal pools. Watch the fiddler crabs scurry for cover as you near, diving in and out of their burrows. They have excellent eyesight. The burrowing of these prodigious creatures stirs up marsh sediments and helps increase the marsh's productivity. Take time to observe their curious behavior.

While you're on Meadow Point, the tide will begin its flood. On this incoming tide, you can begin your paddle back to the launch in

Ockway Bay. Keeping the shore to your right, paddle north to the mouth of Pinquickset Cove. From here make your turn west and paddle across Popponesset Bay, pass Gooseberry Island into Ockway Bay, and back to the launch.

13. *Mashpee River, Mashpee*

Maps:
> USGS Cotuit Quadrangle

Launch location: Pirates Cove Landing, Mashpee Neck Road, Mashpee

Habitats: Bay, tidal river, salt water into brackish

Length of trip: 3 hours

Type of trip: Round-trip paddle with a chance to stop at Farleys Camp upriver and Gooseberry Island on the way back

Paddling distance: 4 miles

Paddling conditions: Protected tidal river with some open bay

Current: Flood in/ebb out. Tide turns 1 hour 30 minutes after launch.

Launch time: On high, same as Boston high

Permits, fees, parking: No permits or fees required to park or launch. Small, paved lot. Off-street parking allowed.

Facilities: No facilities

Handicap access: Paved ramp

Directions to launch: From US 6, take exit 5. Drive on MA 149 south, and then turn right onto MA 28 north. Go 3.5 miles and turn left onto Orchard Road. Drive another 0.5 mile and turn right onto Quinaquisset Avenue. A quick left will take you onto Mashpee Neck Road; it's 1.5 miles to the town landing.

The Tour

The Mashpee River headwaters are at Mashpee-Wakeby Pond. The river winds south for 5 miles and empties into Popponesset Bay. The lower one-third of the river is tidal and encompasses three distinct habitats—freshwater, brackish, and saltwater. It is surrounded by the Mashpee Woodlands Conservation Area, which contains more than 2 miles of maintained trails.

The river plays a major role in the life of the blueback herring. In

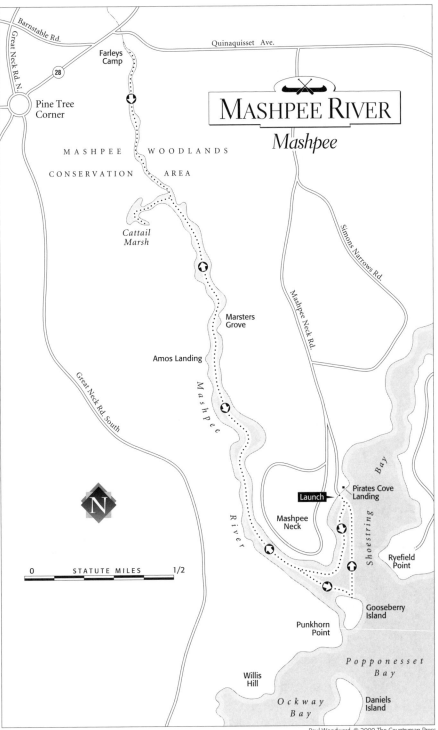

Barnstable Rd.

Great Neck Rd. N.

Quinaquisset Ave.

Farleys Camp

28

Pine Tree Corner

MASHPEE WOODLANDS
CONSERVATION AREA

Cattail Marsh

Simmons Narrows Rd.

Mashpee Neck Rd.

Marsters Grove

Amos Landing

Great Neck Rd South

Mashpee

River

Pirates Cove Landing

Launch

Mashpee Neck

Shoestring

Bay

Ryefield Point

N

0   STATUTE MILES   1/2

Gooseberry Island

Punkhorn Point

Popponesset Bay

Willis Hill

Ockway Bay

Daniels Island

MASHPEE RIVER

Mashpee

spring these anadromous fish use the Mashpee to reach their freshwater spawning grounds. The adults pass through again on their return to salt water in late summer, traveling in schools numbering in the thousands. Those not eaten in the river by shorebirds and snapping turtles are met in Popponesset Bay by hungry bluefish and striped bass.

Begin the trip by launching from the town landing into the flood tide. Keep the shore on your right as you swing around Mashpee Neck and into the mouth of the Mashpee River. Once around the point the current will be with you. For the first mile you will pass a few houses and boats at anchor. This portion is salt water, as evidenced by the cordgrass growing along the shore. The houses begin to disappear, and you know you have entered the Mashpee Woodlands Conservation Area. The Mashpee River Woodland trails, accessible from Marsters Grove on the east side of the river and Amos Landing on the west side, provide an excellent retreat for a walk into a densely forested white pine woodland.

Look for nesting marsh wrens and red-winged blackbirds in the tall grass along the riverbank. Overhead, hear the osprey's call as it circles in search of a meal. A pair of mute swans build their massive nest in the cattail marsh, and by midsummer you may see the mother leading her

*The Mashpee River is an ideal place
to paddle slowly and watch for birds.*

Mute swans cruise the edges of the river.

cygnets. From a distance, the father guards, puffing up his wings and warning you not to venture too close. Other, less territorial residents you may encounter are Canada geese, great blue herons, muskrats, and spotted turtles.

In summer, foraging birds of the river and bay include herring and laughing gulls, common and least terns, snowy egrets, belted king-fishers, and black-crowned night herons. In the fall and winter there are black ducks, buffleheads, and red-breasted mergansers.

Watch for the signs of going over the "wedge" where fresh water and salt water meet: Cattails and bulrushes begin to appear as the salt-marsh grasses disappear. The water is now brackish, and the sides of the river are dominated by narrow-leafed cattail, where you will hear the call of the red-winged blackbird, often referred to as the "song of the marsh." A little farther upstream the water clears and turns colder, and you may find dainty blue forget-me-nots along the banks and mats of emerald green watercress floating below the surface. Other colorful wildflowers such as blue flag iris, jewelweed, and marsh rose line the banks. In this shallow water, you may have to get out of your boat to pull it along, but beware, for the bottom is very mucky in spots, and you could sink in up to your knees.

When you have paddled upriver as far as you can, the entrance to Farleys Camp will be on the left side. Stop here for a break, just as President Grover Cleveland once did when he fished the Mashpee River. The tide should have turned by now, and you can begin your return trip. On your way back, make a stop at Gooseberry Island—a good spot to rest and explore a micro–salt-marsh ecosystem. The island was most likely named after sea gooseberries, or comb jellies, rather than the variety of berry that grows on deciduous shrubs and is preserved in jams and relishes. Once you've explored, paddle back to the launch on Mashpee Neck Road.

14. *Coonamessett Pond, Falmouth*

Maps:
> USGS Falmouth Quadrangle
> USGS Pocasset Quadrangle

Launch location: Hatchville Road, Falmouth
Habitats: Fresh water with wooded pine and oak forest
Length of trip: Open
Type of trip: Round-trip paddle
Paddling distance: 2½ miles
Paddling conditions: Open water
Current: None
Launch time: Anytime
Permits, fees, parking: No parking permits or fees required to use the wooded parking area
Facilities: None
Handicap access: Dirt road with access from sandy shore
Directions to launch: From the Mashpee rotary, at the junction of

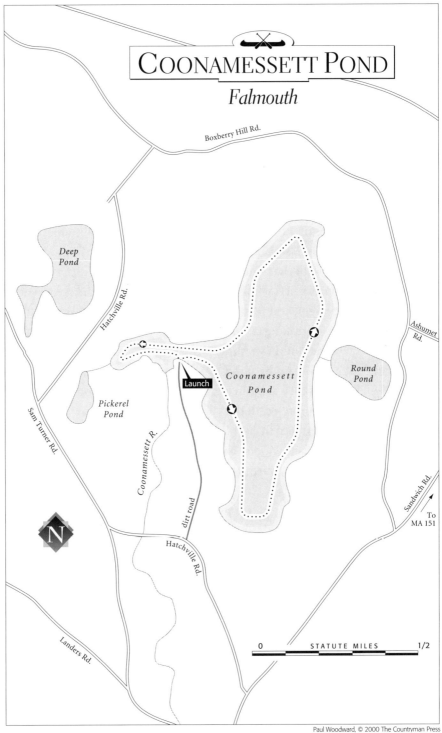

COONAMESSETT POND

Falmouth

Boxberry Hill Rd.

Deep
Pond

Hatchville Rd.

Ashumet
Rd.

Coonamessett
Pond

Round
Pond

Launch

Pickerel
Pond

Sam Turner Rd.

Coonamessett R.

dirt road

N

Hatchville Rd.

Sandwich Rd.

To
MA 151

Landers Rd.

| 0 | STATUTE MILES | 1/2 |

Paul Woodward, © 2000 The Countryman Press

MA 28 and MA 151, take the exit for MA 151 West. Drive 2.5 miles and turn left onto Sandwich Road. In 1.5 miles turn right onto Hatchville Road; in 0.5 mile take another right at the dirt-road entrance to the parking area.

The Pond

Located in Hatchville, this 158-acre freshwater pond has managed to retain its natural beauty because of its isolation. It is sparsely developed as it is the site of a town well and is managed and maintained by the town of Falmouth's Conservation Commission. A dirt road will bring you to the edge of the pond, where you can launch.

It is a quiet place, with very few powerboats (motors are restricted to 6 horsepower), and just the occasional angler casting a line. If you see something breaking the water's surface, it may be a bass, or perhaps a pickerel. The pond is a nursery area for the blueback herring that make their way into the pond by the Coonamessett River. The name *Coonamessett* is said to be an anglicized Algonquian word meaning "at the place for lampreys." In the 1700s the river was known as Five Mile River for the distance from the pond to the sea.

So bring a fishing pole, pack your lunch, don your swimsuit, and enjoy the refreshing, warm waters of tranquil Coonamessett Pond.

15. Mashpee-Wakeby Pond, Mashpee

Maps:
   USGS Sandwich Quadrangle
   USGS Cotuit Quadrangle
Launch location: Fisherman's Landing, Mashpee
Habitat: Freshwater pond
Length of trip: Open
Type of trip: Round-trip paddle with a walk through Lowell-Holly Reservation
Paddling distance: Open
Paddling conditions: Open water, can be choppy during high winds

EVENDEN '99

Pumpkinseeds have a distinctive dark eye-spot near their gills.

Current: None

Launch time: Anytime

Permits, fees, parking: Fisherman's Landing off MA 130 is controlled by state Department of Fisheries and Wildlife. No permits required to park or launch; however, there may be a fee to park during weekends in summer.

Facilities: None

Handicap access: Paved ramp

Directions to launch: From US 6, take exit 3. Turn south onto Quaker Meeting House Road and drive approximately 3.5 miles to MA 130. Turn left (south) onto MA 130, and go 4.3 miles to Landing Road. Turn left, then continue 0.2 mile to the parking lot.

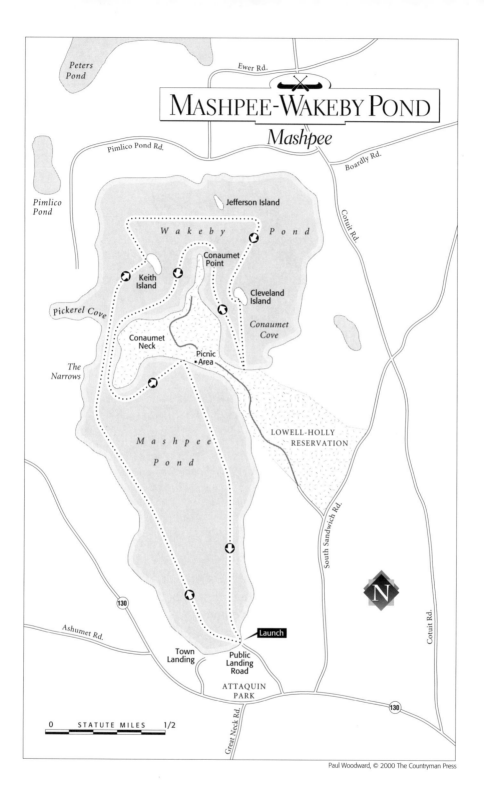

MASHPEE-WAKEBY POND

Mashpee

Peters Pond

Ewer Rd.

Pimlico Pond Rd.

Boardly Rd.

Pimlico Pond

Cotuit Rd.

W a k e b y   P o n d

Jefferson Island

Conaumet Point

Keith Island

Cleveland Island

Pickerel Cove

Conaumet Cove

Conaumet Neck

Picnic Area

The Narrows

M a s h p e e

P o n d

LOWELL-HOLLY RESERVATION

South Sandwich Rd.

N

Cotuit Rd.

130

Ashumet Rd.

Launch

Town Landing

Public Landing Road

ATTAQUIN PARK

Great Neck Rd.

130

0   STATUTE MILES   1/2

Paul Woodward, © 2000 The Countryman Press

EVENDEN '99

Lowell-Holly Reservation contains more than 500 holly trees.

The Pond

Mashpee-Wakeby Pond is the second largest freshwater pond on Cape Cod, with a surface area of 729 acres and depths to 87 feet. Early settlers called it Great Pond, from the Indian name *Mashpee,* meaning great or big waters. In the northern section, Wakeby Pond, are three small, un-inhabited islands—Keith, Jefferson, and Cleveland. They have managed to retain their original trees, including species now rarely seen on Cape Cod such as black birch, hemlock, and witch hazel. However, a species commonly found on the islands, and perhaps what could appropriately be called the official flower of Cape Cod, is poison ivy. Poison ivy does an excellent job of protecting the islands from intruders, as it is a nuisance only to humans. It is a beneficial plant that helps to stabilize soil and provides berries for birds and other wildlife in winter.

On a peninsula jutting into the middle of the pond is the 135-acre Lowell-Holly Reservation, maintained by the Trustees of Reservations. It is a nice place to stop for a picnic or to hike on the trails to view

American beech, rhododendron, and more than 500 holly trees. In summer there is a guide on duty to provide a tour of the reservation.

Mashpee-Wakeby Pond is a popular fishing spot, so be cautious of the many powerboats and jet skis. Early morning is a good time for a paddle as there are fewer powerboats.

Shore shrimp among the rockweed.

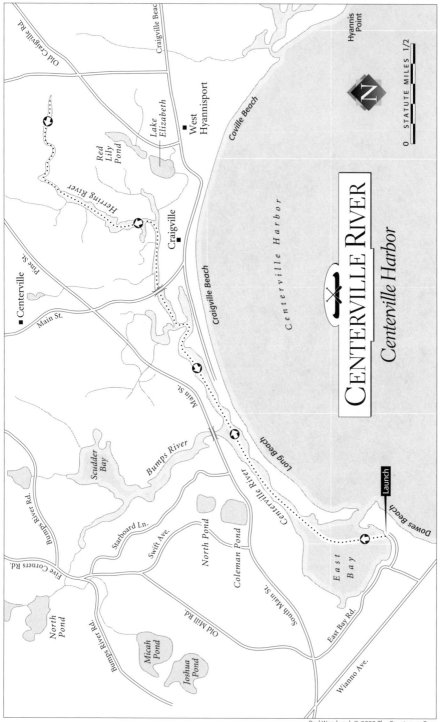

CENTERVILLE RIVER
Centerville Harbor

STATUTE MILES 1/2

0

N

Hyannis
Point

Coville Beach

Centerville Harbor

Craigville Beach

Craigville Beach

Old Craigville Rd.

West
Hyannisport

Lake
Elizabeth

Red
Lily
Pond

Herring River

Craigville

Pine St.

Centerville

Main St.

Long Beach

Dowes Beach

Launch

East
Bay

Centerville River

Bumps River

Scudder
Bay

Bumps River Rd.

Five Corners Rd.

Starboard Ln.

Swift Ave.

North Pond

Coleman Pond

Old Mill Rd.

South Main St.

North
Pond

Bumps River Rd.

Micah
Pond

Joshua
Pond

East Bay Rd.

Wianno Ave.

PART III
Mid-Cape Paddling Tours

16. Centerville River and Scudder Bay, Cotuit (Town of Barnstable)

Maps:
> USGS Hyannis Quadrangle

Launch location: Dowes Town Beach, Osterville

Habitats: Tidal river, bay, barrier beach, salt marsh

Length of trip:
> Centerville River, 4 hours
>
> Scudder Bay, 4 hours

*Paddling the marsh along Salton Point
in Barnstable Harbor*

Type of trip: Round-trip paddle
Paddling distance:
 Centerville River, 6½ miles
 Scudder Bay, 4 miles
Paddling conditions: Flat water on open bay into protected tidal
 river
Current: Flood in/ebb out.
 Centerville River, tide turns at river's end 2 hours 30 minutes
  after launch.
 Scudder Bay, tide turns in Scudder Bay 2 hours 15 minutes
  after launch.
Launch times:
 Centerville River: On high, 45 minutes before Boston high
 Scudder Bay: On high, 45 minutes before Boston high
Permits, fees, parking: No fees to launch. Town of Barnstable
 parking permits required to park during season.
Facilities: None
Handicap access: Paved ramp
Directions to launch: From US 6, take exit 5 and drive on MA 149
 south to MA 28. Turn left onto MA 28 and drive 0.5 mile, then
 turn right onto South County Road, which becomes Main Street.
 After 2.4 miles turn right onto East Bay Road. (***Note:*** Be sure to
 bear left at Wianno Avenue and Main Street intersections.) In 0.7
 mile you'll see the entrance to Dowes Beach, behind a white
 picket fence. Turn in and drive 0.3 mile to the beach parking lot.

The Tour

Launch from Dowes Beach in Osterville and paddle across East Bay into the Centerville River. After paddling for ½ mile behind a long beach you will have the choice of either continuing on the Centerville or going left on the Bumps River and into Scudder Bay. Both trips take about 3½ to 4 hours to paddle, but the Scudder Bay trip is only half the distance of the Centerville River one, which means you can paddle at a more leisurely pace. Both routes are pleasant in spring and fall. In spring, wintering-over sea ducks are still here, and in late summer, the migratory birds have not yet left. During the summer, however, the trip of

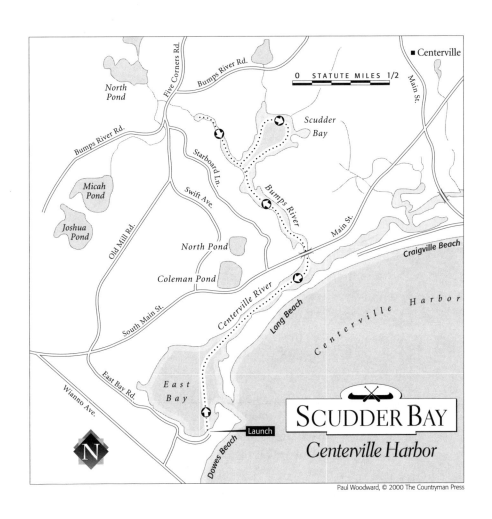

North Pond

Five Corners Rd.

Bumps River Rd.

■ Centerville

0 STATUTE MILES 1/2

Main St.

Scudder Bay

Bumps River Rd.

Starboard Ln.

Micah Pond

Swift Ave.

Joshua Pond

Old Mill Rd.

North Pond

Bumps River

Main St.

Coleman Pond

Craigville Beach

South Main St.

Centerville River

Long Beach

Centerville Harbor

East Bay Rd.

East Bay

Wianno Ave.

N

Dowes Beach

Launch

SCUDDER BAY

Centerville Harbor

Paul Woodward, © 2000 The Countryman Press

*Male buffleheads have a large white patch on their heads;
females have a much smaller one under the eye.*

choice for relative peace and quiet would be Scudder Bay. The Centerville River in the Craigville Beach area is very busy and noisy from Memorial Day weekend on through August.

Paddle up the Bumps River and across Scudder Bay to the freshwater section of the river. You cannot get very far up the river, but it is a nice place to paddle into, sit in your boat, and smell the heady aroma of marsh roses. After a healthy whiff of roses, paddle back into Scudder Bay, keeping the shore to your right, and float into an inlet that will end in ½ mile at Bumps River Road. This is a quiet spot of brackish water; cattails and red maples grow on the banks. When the tide turns, keep the shore to your right as you paddle out the Bumps River and back to East Bay.

If you choose to paddle the Centerville River, follow the flow of the river as it takes you from East Bay, down behind Craigville Beach, and out into the marshes of the Herring River. If you follow the Herring all the way to the end, it is a steady, but not overly tiring paddle. At the very end, in overgrown phragmites (common reeds) and brackish water, wait for the tide change and then return to Dowes Beach.

17. *Osterville Grand Island, Cotuit (Town of Barnstable)*

Maps:
> USGS Cotuit Quadrangle

Launch location: Old Shore Road, Cotuit

Habitats: Saltwater bay, large island

Length of trip: 4 hours

Type of trip: Round-trip paddle

Paddling distance: 6 miles

Paddling conditions: Flat water on open bay

Current: Ebb out/flood in. Tide turns at Sampsons Island 3 hours after launch.

Launch time: On low, 2 hours 15 minutes before Boston low

Permits, fees, parking: Parking lot restricted to cars with Barnstable resident beach permits; no launching fee. Streetside parking permitted.

Facilities: None

Handicap access: Sand ramp

Directions to launch: Take exit 5 off US 6 and turn onto MA 149 south. Drive to the intersection with MA 28, turn right, and go 0.5 mile on MA 28 until you come to Putnam Avenue. Turn left, drive 1.9 miles, and turn left onto Old Shore Road. It's just a short distance to the town landing.

The Tour

This trip around Osterville Grand Island will take you across three bays—Cotuit, North, and West—and along the Seapuit River on the back side of Sampsons Island. Plan to begin your trip a few hours before low tide, and you will have an incoming tide for your return along the Seapuit. You can circumnavigate the island either way, but going left to North Bay, then south to West Bay, and west through the Seapuit River will mean both an incoming tide and the prevailing southwest winds at your back on the way home.

The Old Shore Road launch location provides easy access to the water but restricted parking. Busy little Oyster Harbors, not surpris-

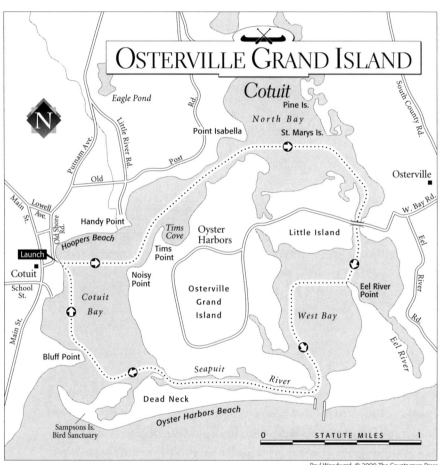

OSTERVILLE GRAND ISLAND

Cotuit

Eagle Pond

Putnam Ave.

Little River Rd.

Rd.

Post

Old

Lowell Ave.

Main St.

Old Shore Rd.

School St.

Main St.

Pine Is.

North Bay

Point Isabella

St. Marys Is.

South County Rd.

Osterville

W. Bay Rd.

Handy Point

Hoopers Beach

Tims Cove

Oyster Harbors

Little Island

Eel River Point

Eel River

Tims Point

Noisy Point

Cotuit Bay

Osterville Grand Island

West Bay

Eel River Rd.

Launch

Cotuit

Bluff Point

Sampsons Is.
Bird Sanctuary

Seapuit   River

Dead Neck

Oyster Harbors Beach

0   STATUTE MILES   1

Paul Woodward, © 2000 The Countryman Press

EVENDEN '99

The common oyster was once very plentiful in this area.

ingly named for the abundance of oysters once harvested here, hosts a number of different watercraft, from sleek rowing sculls to working scallopers. Dead ahead from the launch is Osterville Grand Island; Sampsons Island is to the right. Osterville Grand Island is an appropriate name, for it is a place of grand homes with luxuriously landscaped gardens stretching to the bay. This trip is for observing not birds and other wildlife, but the homes and boats of the well-to-do.

As you make your way into North Bay, stay on a southeasterly tack around Little Island, which is part of Grand Island. Avoid the boat channel, as from here on a parade of boats of various sizes passes under the drawbridge (the only bridge connecting the island with the mainland) as they navigate through West Bay, en route to Nantucket Sound. Once under the bridge and in West Bay, if you are sorely in need of a stretching break, pull over to the left, at Eel River Point. This is also an opportunity to do some beachcombing. The last leg of your trip is around the southeasterly point of Grand Island. Here you will feel the wind in your face, so stay close to the right shore as you enter the Seapuit River. On the east end of Sampsons Island is Dead Neck, a good place to stop for a swim from Oyster Harbors Beach and wait for the

Oyster Harbor offers great paddling for all ages.

tide to turn. Sampsons Island is owned and managed by the Massachusetts Audubon Society, and access is prohibited without a special permit. From your boat you can observe a variety of shorebirds such as piping plovers, sandpipers, terns, and gulls, all harmoniously foraging along the beach. With the tide, float downriver past elegant homes with security cameras disguised as birdhouses following your every movement. As you leave the river, cautiously head straight across Cotuit Bay, as you will be traversing a busy boat channel. Once across the channel, stay close to the shore, now out of the wind and able to make your way back to the takeout, again through a maze of boats.

18. *Barnstable Great Marsh, Barnstable*

Maps:
  USGS Hyannis Quadrangle
Launch location: Blish Point State Landing, Barnstable
Habitats: Bay, salt marsh, tidal creeks, tide pools
Length of trip: 5¼ hours
Type of trip: Round-trip paddle with a walk on the marsh
Paddling distance: 10 miles

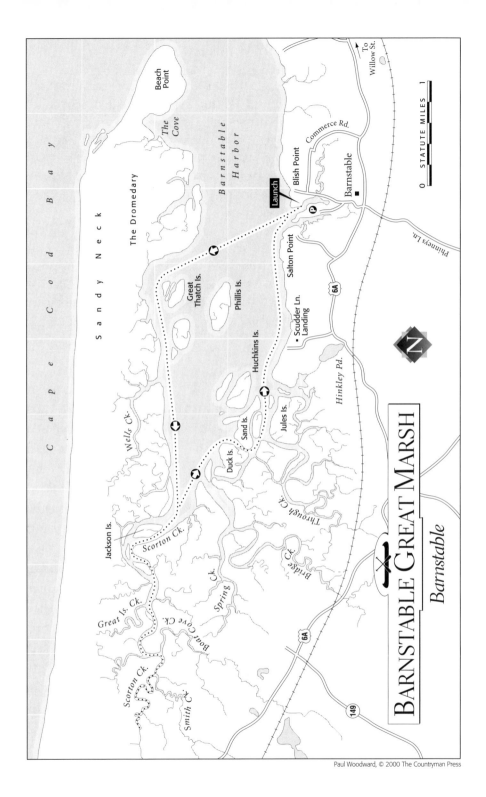

Cape Cod Bay

Sandy Neck

The Dromedary

Beach Point

The Cove

Barnstable Harbor

Blish Point

Commerce Rd.

To Willow St.

Barnstable

Launch

Salton Point

Scudder Ln. Landing

6A

Phinneys Ln.

Great Thatch Is.

Phillis Is.

Huchkins Is.

Sand Is.

Jules Is.

Hinkley Pd.

Duck Is.

Wells Ck.

Through Ck.

Jackson Is.

Scorton Ck.

Spring Ck.

Bridge Ck.

Great Is. Ck.

Boat Cove Ck.

Scorton Ck.

Smith Ck.

6A

149

N

0   STATUTE MILES   1

BARNSTABLE GREAT MARSH

Barnstable

Paddling conditions: Open bay into tidal river and marsh creeks
Current: Flood in/ebb out. Tide turns at western end of Scorton Creek 3 hours 15 minutes after launch.
Launch time: On high, 2 hours 15 minutes before Boston high
Permits, fees, parking: No permits required to park at dirt lot located at south end of marina (see map). Parking fee for trailers only at state landing, where you can unload if car-topping, but may not park.
Facilities: Portable toilet
Handicap access: Paved ramp
Directions to launch: From US 6, take exit 7 and drive along Willow Street north to MA 6A. Turn left onto MA 6A west, and after 2.4 miles turn right onto Millway Road. It's 0.3 mile to a parking lot at the south end of the marina.

The Tour

Barnstable Great Marsh is the largest salt marsh on Cape Cod, encompassing more than 4,000 acres. This marsh began forming more than 4,000 years ago and now has peat as deep as 30 feet. Only the highest of tides—those that occur during a new or full moon—are able to reach back into this massive maze of creeks and flood the salt-marsh hay *(Spartina patens)* in the high marsh. Cordgrass *(Spartina alterniflora)*, the building block of a salt marsh, is the tall grass growing along the creek edges. This tour will take you into the heart of a salt marsh, a most productive coastal marine environment.

There is so much to see, but first we need to launch. This trip can only be navigated at high tide. There is an 8- to 12-foot tidal range, which means that at low tide you will get hung up on sandflats. There are two options for a put-in: If you have enough water, launch at the creek on the west side of the entrance to the harbor, which will keep you out of the busy inner harbor boat traffic. When the tide is a little lower, launch from the state landing at Blish Point. Once you are launched and out in the harbor, take time to get your bearings. To the north is Sandy Neck, a 7-mile barrier beach protecting the Great Marsh from Cape Cod Bay.

The willet shows its distinctive black-and-white wing pattern in flight.

On a northwest tack, head for The Dromedary—a hump of sand the color of a camel—on Sandy Neck. Once across the harbor you will paddle by, or over, islands of grass with fitting names like Little Thatch Island and Great Thatch Island. Turn west now, paddle over to Jackson Island, and stop for a short break before beginning the lengthy paddle up Scorton Creek. Scorton Creek is about 4 miles long with many tributaries to explore. Take your time to stop, look, and listen. Paddle up close to the cordgrass and watch salt-marsh snails scurry up the grass as the tide approaches. Below the cordgrass ribbed mussels are found attached to the peat, filtering organic matter from the water. You may see a hustling movement on the marsh as the most easily identifiable crab—the fiddler crab, aptly named for the male's huge right claw—scurries in and out of its burrow, turning over sediments and increasing the soil's productivity. Just like a garden rototiller! Take a break on the marsh and walk into the high marsh area to feel the softness of salt-marsh hay underfoot. For a natural food treat, sample a glasswort. The most common glasswort found on the marsh is sea pickle, a crispy, edible succulent with a salty taste.

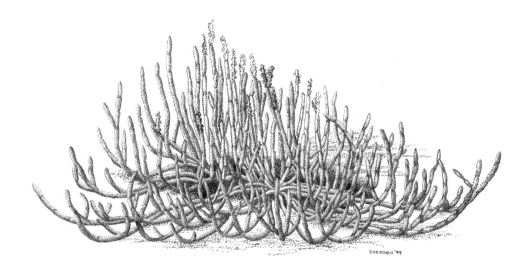

Sea pickle, a glasswort, grows in the salt marsh.

Watch for the turning tide, for as the water pours out of the Great Marsh all these creeks will become dry except for the many damp feet of marsh muck below. Paddle out of Scorton creek while you still can and head southeast to Scudder Lane (a town landing with boats moored nearby at the Barnstable Yacht Club). Follow the flow of the water as it drains the creeks. If you find yourself going against the flow in any of the creeks, then you will need to reverse your direction. Scudder Lane Landing will be a welcome rest stop before you begin the journey back to the launch.

For another day's trip, head southwest from the launch and paddle into either Spring or Through Creek, and see how far back you can get into the many tributaries feeding into the harbor.

19. *Barnstable Harbor to Sandy Neck, Barnstable*

Maps:
   USGS Hyannis Quadrangle
Launch location: Blish Point State Landing, Barnstable
Habitats: Bay, sand dunes on barrier beach
Length of trips:
   The Dromedary, 4 hours
   Beach Point, 3½ hours
Type of trip: Round-trip paddle and walk on Sandy Neck
Paddling distances:
   The Dromedary, 5 miles
   Beach Point, 6 miles
Paddling conditions: Open bay, could be choppy if winds are
   10 knots or more
Current:
   The Dromedary, flood in/ebb out. Tide turns at The Dromedary
      2 hours 45 minutes after launch.
   Beach Point, ebb out/flood in. Tide turns at Beach Point 2 hours
      45 minutes after launch.
Launch times:
   The Dromedary, on high, 2½ hours before Boston high
   Beach Point, on low, 2½ hours before Boston low

Permits, fees, parking: A fee for trailer parking only at state landing. No launch fees. Off-street automobile parking available at south end of marina. Ask attendant for advice about parking.

Facilities: Portable toilet

Handicap access: Paved ramp

Directions to launch: From US 6, take exit 7 and go north on Willow Street north to MA 6A. Turn left onto MA 6A west, and after 2.4 miles turn right onto Millway Road. It's 0.3 mile to a parking lot, Blish Point State Landing, at the north end of the marina.

The Tour

Sandy Neck is a 7-mile-long, breathtaking barrier beach with the second highest sand dunes on the Cape (the highest are in the Province Lands in Provincetown). The neck is accessible on foot from the conservation area entrance on Sandy Neck Road in Sandwich; however, the best way to experience it is by boat, paddling across Barnstable Harbor. After launching and heading into the harbor, one can appreciate the full magnificence of the dunes looming north and dead ahead. On a sunny day they light up the harbor with their glow.

These paddlers hug the shore along Sandy Neck.

Peaceful seclusion can be found on Sandy Neck.

The Dromedary

Paddle across the harbor, with the massive hump of a sand dune, fittingly called The Dromedary, as your reference point to the northwest. Keep your eyes open along the way for schools of small fish such as silversides or mummichogs breaking to the surface as the larger bluefish and striped bass pursue them from below. Overhead, you are likely to see herring and blackback gulls and common terns displaying a feeding frenzy; the little fish leap to the surface to escape the big fish below, only to be snatched by the birds from above.

Once you reach the opposite shore, take out on the salt marsh, being sure to haul your boat up to the wrack line, the line where rockweed and other seaweed are left behind as the tide ebbs, as the tidal range here is 12 feet. Take a walk on the paths through the dunes. You are likely to find total solitude here, except for a couple of fishing and hunting shacks tucked into the dunes. A limited number of permits are issued to four-wheel-drive vehicles for passage on the two unpaved roads—the marsh road, which floods at high tide, and the road through the dunes, which leads to the village at Beach Point on the eastern end of Sandy Neck. Stay on the trails and make your way up the dunes to the top. On a clear day, looking northeast, you can see the Pilgrim Monument in Provincetown. To the southwest take in the expansive emerald green of Barnstable Great Marsh. On your hike look for Indian middens, piles of shells discarded by the Matakeese and Cummaquid Indians who lived in this area prior to the 1600s.

Many plants thrive in this impoverished sandy soil, the most conspicuous of which is American beach grass. Its rigid stems stand upright, and when the wind blows, the outer blades bend and leave a picturesque pattern of circles around each plant. Beach grass aids in dune stabilization by sending out rhizomes (or runners) horizontally. Another prominent dune plant, spreading like a carpet over the sand, is poverty grass or beach heather. But the most profuse plant, shining in the sun, is poison ivy, growing among the bayberry and beach plum bushes. In spring beach plum is easily identified by its plumelike display of small white flowers; in the fall the plant's fruits mature into reddish-purple plums, highly coveted for jellies and jams.

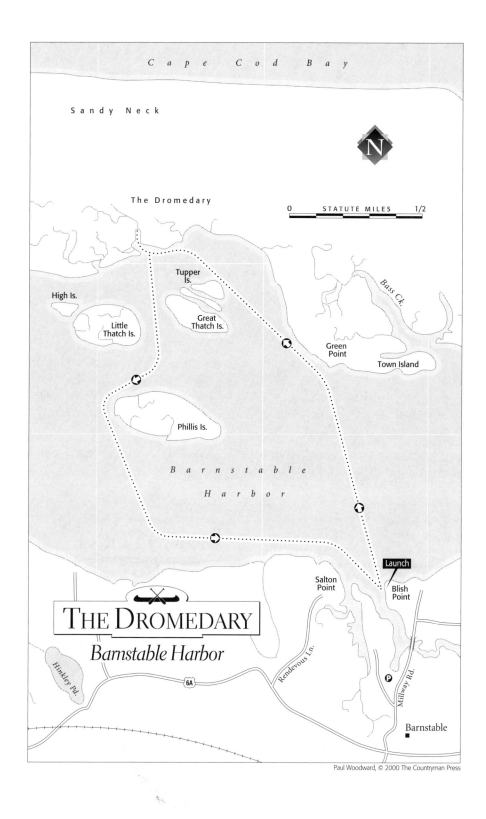

Cape Cod Bay

Sandy Neck

The Dromedary

0   STATUTE MILES   1/2

High Is.

Tupper Is.

Little Thatch Is.

Great Thatch Is.

Bass Ck.

Green Point

Town Island

Phillis Is.

Barnstable

Harbor

Launch

Salton Point

Blish Point

THE DROMEDARY

Barnstable Harbor

Hinkley Pd.

Rendevous Ln.

6A

Millway Rd.

Barnstable

Paul Woodward, © 2000 The Countryman Press

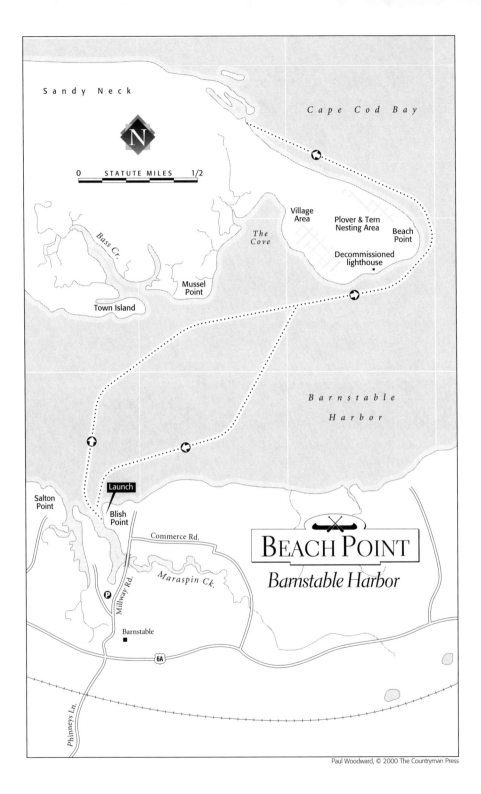

Sandy Neck

Cape Cod Bay

STATUTE MILES
0   1/2

Bass Cr.

The Cove

Village Area

Plover & Tern Nesting Area

Beach Point

Decommissioned lighthouse

Mussel Point

Town Island

Barnstable Harbor

Salton Point

Launch

Blish Point

Commerce Rd.

Maraspin Ck.

Millway Rd.

Barnstable

6A

Phinneys Ln.

BEACH POINT

Barnstable Harbor

Paul Woodward, © 2000 The Countryman Press

For the return trip, head southwest and take a rest break at Little Thatch Island before you embark on the 1½-mile paddle across the harbor. On the opposite side, keep the shore to your right as you paddle back to the launch area, passing the impressive fleet of wooden catboats anchored in the harbor of the West Barnstable Yacht Club.

Beach Point

On the far easternmost tip of Sandy Neck lies Beach Point, a good trip if the tide is out and sandflats restrict passage in the harbor. From Blish Point, follow the boat channel east, past the private village of summer cottages, to the public shore beyond the lighthouse, where you can take out and explore the flats. The early 1900s cedar-shingled cottages of this quaint colony lie cloistered in their own little world, devoid of electricity, telephone, and paved roads. Vehicular access over land is restricted to permitted vehicles only and is closely regulated during piping plover nesting season. The lighthouse, now minus its light, was decommissioned in the 1930s when the commercial fishing industry dwindled and, with it, the need for a navigational beacon on the shore.

The farthest point of Sandy Neck, where the harbor opens into Cape Cod Bay, is where many recreational fishing boats congregate. With an incoming tide, it will be an easy paddle back to the launch with plenty of water to skirt the boat channel.

There is often a good deal of boat traffic through Barnstable Harbor during the day; however, it is a spectacular spot for a late afternoon paddle, with the sun setting in the west on the return trip.

20. *Chase Garden Creek, Yarmouthport*

Maps:
  USGS Dennis Quadrangle
Launch location: Grays Beach, Center Street in Yarmouthport
Habitats: Salt marsh, tidal creek
Length of trip: 4 hours
Type of trip: Round-trip paddle with a stop on the marsh
Paddling distance: 6 miles
Paddling conditions: Flat water on quick-flowing, meandering tidal creek

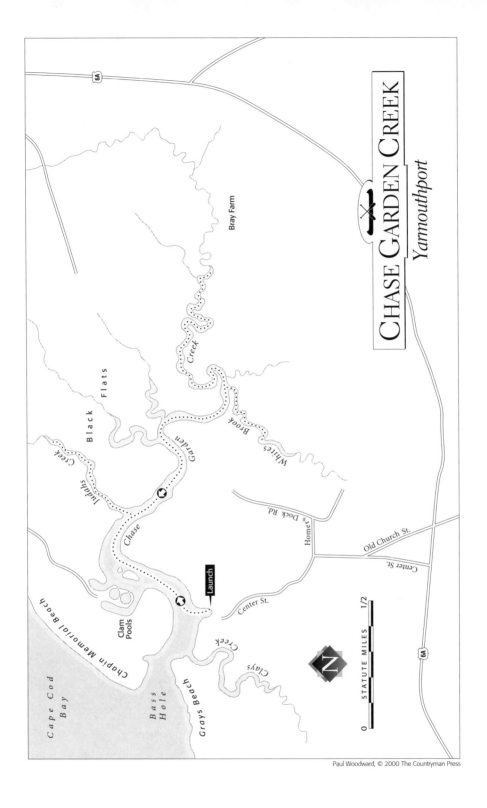

CHASE GARDEN CREEK
Yarmouthport

Bray Farm

Creek

Black Flats

Judahs Creek

Creek

Garden

Whites Brook

Chase

Homers Dock Rd.

Old Church St.

Center St.

Center St.

Launch

Clam Pools

Chapin Memorial Beach

Cape Cod Bay

Bass Hole

Grays Beach

Clays Creek

N

STATUTE MILES

0   1/2

6A

6A

Current: Flood in/ebb out. Tide turns in marsh 2 hours after launch.

Launch time: On high, 1 hour before Boston high

Permits, fees, parking: No fees or permits required to park or launch. Large, paved lot.

Facilities: Rest rooms and picnic tables

Handicap access: Paved ramp

Directions to launch: From exit 8 off US 6, take Union Street north to MA 6A, cross MA 6A onto Old Church Street, and drive 0.3 mile. Turn right onto Center Street and bear left at the intersection with Homer's Dock Road. It's 0.9 mile to the parking lot.

The Tour

Chase Garden Creek is a long, broad creek that meanders inland for about 3 miles. Two major tributaries, Judahs and Whites Brooks, feed into it. At the mouth of Chase Garden is Bass Hole, where in the 1700s ships were built and then launched into Cape Cod Bay. This trip will not take the route of those great ships but will follow the route of schools of small fish, such as minnows and silversides, that make their home in the creeks and are a source of food for larger fish entering on the incoming tide.

Launch from Grays Beach on an incoming tide, stay to your right, and at about the ½-mile point, head north and make a trip into Judahs Creek.

Judahs Creek

Judahs Creek is about ½ mile long. There is a very impressive osprey nest up on a platform in the marsh. The size of the nest reveals that this pair of osprey have been returning to this site for a number of years, continuing to replenish the nest with discards not just from nature, but from civilization as well—plastics carelessly disposed of from boats and shore. After you've had a look, turn around and head back to the main creek (you will have the current against you at this time).

Once back on Chase Garden Creek, go with the flow and follow it to the end, where you will see Bray Farm, a working farm that also hosts a number of trails overlooking the marsh. Make a stop on the marsh to observe the diversity of plants. What appears to be an expanse of grass

Platforms provide nesting places for the osprey.

EVENDEN '99

You can just make out the osprey perched on its nest.

is made up of not only the dominant cordgrass and salt-marsh hay, but also of succulents such as woody glassworts, and one of the most beautiful marsh plants to bloom in late summer: sea lavender *(Limnomium nashii)*. Sea lavender has become increasingly scarce because of the decline in salt marshes and the plant's popularity in dried flower arrangements. The tide should have turned while you explored the marsh, and you can begin your return journey.

As you pass Judahs Creek on your way back to the launch, stay to the right and you will pass a shellfish processing plant and an area that at low tide is all sandflats.

Whites Brook

An alternate route, Whites Brook, is accessible from Chase Garden Creek. The brook was named for Jonathan White, the first Pilgrim child born in New England. Paddle up Whites to the little creek that flows out of Tom Matthews Pond. You will not be able to paddle into the pond, but you will see the influence of fresh water on the vegetation as plants such as cattails begin to appear. When the tide turns, you can paddle back to the launch.

21. *Bass River, Dennis*

Maps:
> USGS Dennis Quadrangle

Launch locations:
> Bass River North, Cove Road
> Bass River South, Follins Pond Road

Habitats: Tidal river, salt pond, upland woods

Length of trips:
> One-way, 4 hours
> Round-trip, 3 hours

Type of trip: One-way or round-trip paddle and walk

Paddling distances:
> One-way, 5 miles
> Round trip, 3 miles

Paddling conditions: Open tidal river

Current:
> Bass River North, one-way, flood in. Tide turns at Follins Pond 4½ hours after launch.
> Bass River North, round trip, flood in/ebb out. Tide turns at Indian Lands 1 hour 30 minutes after launch.
> Bass River South, one-way, ebb out. Tide turns at Grand Cove 4½ hours after launch.

Launch times:
> Bass River North, one-way, on high, 2 hours 45 minutes before Boston high
> Bass River North, round trip, on high, same as Boston high
> Bass River South, one-way, on high, 2 hours 30 minutes after Boston high

Permits, fees, parking: No permits or fees required to park or launch. Both launches have medium-sized, dirt parking lots.

Facilities: None

Handicap access: Paved ramps

Directions to launches: To get to Cove Road Landing from US 6, take exit 9. Turn onto MA 134 south and drive 0.7 mile, then make a right onto Upper County Road. In 0.2 mile turn left onto Main Street. Drive 0.6 mile and turn right onto Cove Road. Go 0.6 mile to the town landing.

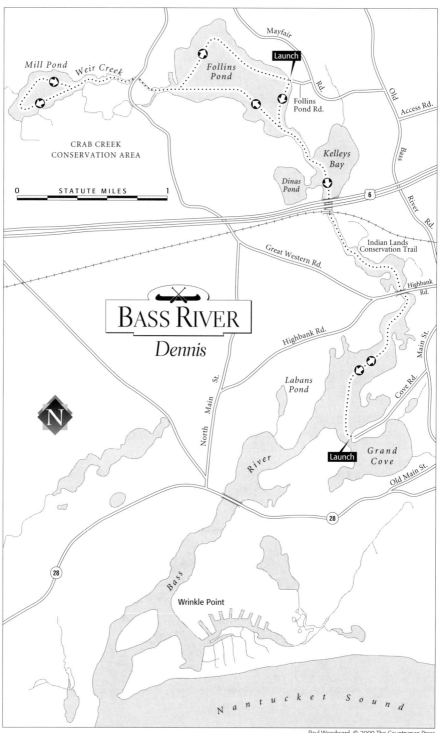

Mayfair

Launch

Mill Pond

Weir Creek

Follins Pond

Follins Pond Rd.

Rd.

Old

Access Rd.

CRAB CREEK
CONSERVATION AREA

Kelleys
Bay

Bass

0   STATUTE MILES   1

Dinas
Pond

6

River

Rd.

Great Western Rd.

Indian Lands
Conservation Trail

Highbank
Rd.

✕
BASS RIVER

Dennis

Highbank Rd.

Main St.

N

Labans
Pond

North Main St.

Cove Rd.

River

Launch

*Grand
Cove*

Old Main St.

28

Bass

River

28

Wrinkle Point

N a n t u c k e t   S o u n d

Follins Pond Road Landing: Take MA 134 north from exit 9 off US 6, and in 0.3 mile turn left onto Access Road. In another 0.3 mile turn right onto Old Bass River Road. Drive for 0.5 mile, turn left onto Mayfair Road, then travel another 0.5 mile to turn left onto Follins Pond Road (be careful not to confuse Follins Bay Road with Follins Pond Road). It's 0.2 mile to the town landing.

The Tour

The Bass River is the longest river on the Cape. From Nantucket Sound to Mill Pond is a 7-mile journey. The greatest tidal influence is felt from the sound north to Kelleys Bay, where you pass under the railroad and US 6 bridges. The river south of MA 28 in Dennis is very busy with boat traffic from the many town landings that provide quick access to the sound, therefore the trip we describe begins and ends north of MA 28.

Bass River North

Launch from Cove Road in South Dennis and paddle upriver. The prevailing southwest wind will be at your back, helping you along. About a mile upriver you will pass under Highbank–Great Western Road, but continue for another ¼ mile where you can stop for a walk along the 2-

mile Indian Lands Conservation Trail that skirts the bank of the river. It is a peaceful spot to view wildflowers and woodland birds. Keep your eyes open for the occasional Native American artifact unearthed after a rainstorm. If you wish, you can paddle into the salt pond in the conservation lands for a look at a salt marsh.

If you are making this a round-trip paddle, it is now time to return to the launch. If you have spotted a car at the Follins Pond Road landing and you're on a one-way paddle, it is time to get back in your boat and head upriver. From here the river narrows and the tidal influence is felt the most keenly. You'll find quick water with a stiff current under the bridges into Kelleys Bay. Once in the bay, the river widens, the current slows, and you can return to a more relaxed paddling stroke. The river will again narrow as it enters Follins Pond.

Archaeological evidence links the Bass river with a visit by Leif Eriksson around A.D. 1000. Excavations in a gully along the pond turned up evidence of what might have been a Norse boat shed. A few boulders with holes resembling Norse mooring holes were found in the pond; other details of his visit still remain a mystery.

Follins Pond and Mill Pond, joined by Weir Creek, form the headwaters of the Bass River. The brook is named for the traps or dams once set out in the ponds to catch fish. The brook passes through a stone-lined culvert. If you've got enough water, you may be able to pull yourself through to enter Mill Pond. On the southern shore of the pond is Crab Creek Conservation Area, named for the abundance of blue crabs found here. There is also a trail through the woodlands that passes an old cranberry bog.

Paddle around the pond and then back through the culvert and into Follins Pond. Take out at the town landing on Follins Pond Road, located on the east side of the pond before it channels into Kelleys Bay.

Bass River South

Using the appropriate launch times, you can reverse this trip, putting your boat in at Follins Pond Road and paddling to Cove Road for a one-way trip.

22. *Herring River, West Harwich*

Maps:
> USGS Harwich Quadrangle

Launch locations:
> MA 28, West Harwich (Coy Brook and East Reservoir)
>
> Bells Neck Road, West Harwich (West Reservoir)

Habitats: Freshwater kettle pond, salt marshes, brackish cattail marsh

Length of trips:
> Coy Brook, 3½ hours
>
> East Reservoir, 3 hours
>
> Bells Neck North, 2½ hours
>
> Bells Neck South, 4 hours

Types of trip:
> Coy Brook, round-trip paddle
>
> East Reservoir, round-trip paddle
>
> Bells Neck North, one-way paddle
>
> Bells Neck South, one-way paddle

Paddling distances:
> Coy Brook, 5 miles
>
> East Reservoir, 3½ miles
>
> Bells Neck North, 2 miles
>
> Bells Neck South, 4½ miles

Paddling conditions: Open, small kettle pond and sheltered tidal river

Current:
> Coy Brook, flood in/ebb out. Tide turns in Coy's Brook 2 hours after launch.
>
> East Reservoir, flood in/ebb out. Tide turns in East Reservoir 1 hour 45 minutes after launch.
>
> Bells Neck North, ebb out. Tide turns at dike 1 hour after launch.
>
> Bells Neck South, ebb out. Tide turns at dike 1 hour 15 minutes after launch.

Launch times:
> Coy Brook, on high, same as Boston high
>
> East Reservoir, on high, 15 minutes before Boston high
>
> Bells Neck North, on high, 1 hour after Boston high

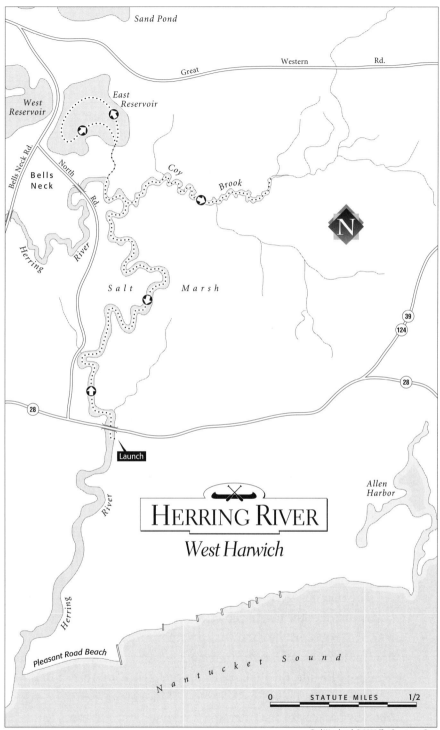

Sand Pond

Great   Western   Rd.

West
Reservoir

East
Reservoir

Bells Neck Rd.

Bells
Neck

North Rd.

Coy   Brook

Herring

River

Salt   Marsh

39
124

28

28

Launch

Herring River

Allen
Harbor

HERRING RIVER

West Harwich

Herring River

Pleasant Road Beach

N a n t u c k e t   S o u n d

0   STATUTE MILES   1/2

Paul Woodward, © 2000 The Countryman Press

Bells Neck South, on high, 45 minutes after Boston high

Permits, fees, parking: No permits or fees required to park or launch from Bells Neck Road or MA 28

Facilities: No facilities

Handicap access: Paved ramp at MA 28, dirt launch from Bells Neck Road. A carryover is required at dike.

Directions to launch: To get to Bells Neck Road, take exit 10 from US 6 and turn onto MA 124 south. Drive to the intersection of MA 124 and MA 39 and turn right onto Great Western Road (also called Main Street). Drive 2 miles, and turn left onto Bells Neck Road. It's 0.2 mile to the West Reservoir launch.

To get to the MA 28 launch, take exit 10 from US 6 and turn onto MA 124 south. Drive to the intersection of MA 124 and MA 39. Take MA 39 south for 1.3 miles to MA 28, turn right onto MA 28 north, go 0.9 mile, and turn left onto the town landing just before the Herring River bridge.

The Tours

The Herring River in West Harwich has to be Cape Cod's equivalent of a "Massachusetts Wild and Scenic River." Thanks to the foresight of the town of Harwich, much of the land surrounding the river and the reservoirs is protected. The Harwich Conservation Lands consist of more than 245 acres of tidal creeks and marshes, a herring run, two kettle ponds (East and West Reservoirs), and several miles of foot trails through woodlands. The Herring River encompasses a multitude of habitats and allows you to paddle from salt water to brackish water, salt marsh to cattail marsh, and salt water to fresh water, in less than 4 miles.

The Herring River is tidal up to the dike where a manufactured fish ladder provides the herring access to the fresh water in the West Reservoir. This trip must be coordinated with the tides to have ample water to reach the dike. There are two major launch locations. Your choice depends on the tide, the time, and your preference for upriver or downriver travel. There is also the option of making this a round-trip or one-way paddle; for the latter, spot a second vehicle at the takeout.

The footbridge at North Road
provides easy access to the Herring River.

MA 28 *Launch*

Launch on an incoming tide and pass under the MA 28 bridge heading north (see Herring River map). A few houses on the western shore are the last signs of people as the river winds through a salt marsh. This is an active spot for birds; many feed on the marshes, and some make it their home. Scan the sky for osprey circling overhead—with a wingspan of more than 6 feet, they are easy to identify. Great blue herons and snowy egrets are found on the marsh, feeding on fish and crustaceans. If you are quiet, you may be able to get up close and watch these birds gracefully stalking their prey. Also seen on the marsh in the spring are nesting Canada geese.

Before the river begins to turn west, go east and paddle into the broad creek called Coy Brook. Paddle to the end, where you can take a break on the marsh and wait for the tide to turn before returning to the launch. From MA 28 up to the head of Coy Brook and back is about a 5-mile paddle.

An alternate route is to paddle into East Reservoir. Continue west on the Herring River, pass the entrance to Coy Brook, and before the

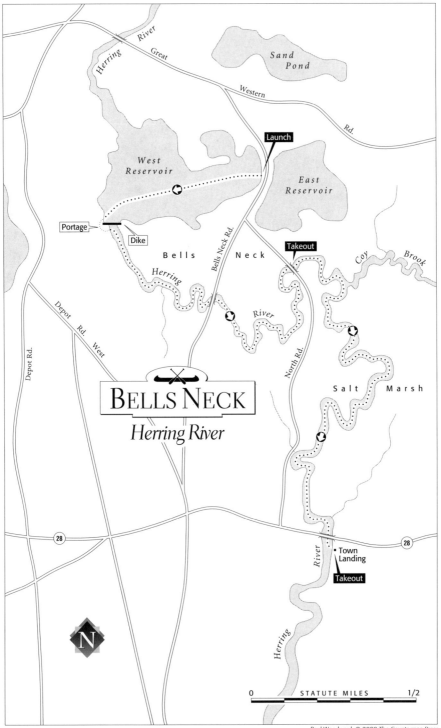

Herring River

Great

Sand Pond

Western

Rd.

Launch

West Reservoir

East Reservoir

Portage

Dike

Bells Neck

Takeout

Coy Brook

Herring

Bells Neck Rd.

River

Depot Rd. West

North Rd.

Salt Marsh

Depot Rd.

BELLS NECK

Herring River

28

28

River

Town Landing

Takeout

Herring

N

0 STATUTE MILES 1/2

footbridge, notice a creek that flows (as the tide floods) into the East Reservoir. Take care that you don't get hung up on the remains of an old metal floodgate. This old gate you just passed was once used to trap fresh water for cranberry bogs in the area. East and West Reservoirs are not used for drinking water but for the bogs. East Reservoir (brackish) and West Reservoir (fresh water) are both fairly deep and surrounded by black and white oaks, pitch pine, and tupelo. Aquatic plants include pickerelweed, with their showy violet-blue spiky flowers, and arrow arum, with large, triangular-shaped, fleshy leaves resembling arrows. Both reservoirs are home to numerous mute swans and the black-crowned night-heron. The tide will turn while you are exploring the East Reservoir; you can then paddle on an outgoing tide back to the launch.

Bells Neck Road Launch

For another paddle (see Bells Neck map), launch from the shore at Bells Neck Road into the West Reservoir. Paddle through the maze of tree stumps, the remains of trees that died when the area was flooded. Take care not to get hung up on the ones just below the surface. As you paddle past the stumps you will probably hear the splash of painted turtles jumping into the water for cover; there is a large population of them here. The serpentine-necked, black bird with an orange throat pouch, perched upon a stump with its wings spread open, is a double-crested cormorant. Cormorants dive underwater for fish, and the lack of oil glands to waterproof their feathers necessitates their rather staturesque appearance as they spread their wings to dry. Across the reservoir on the left you will see the dike. You can take out either to the right or left of the dike.

You will now need to put in on the Herring River. There is a launch from the bank beside the overflow culvert and another from the wall on the opposite side. In spring the fish ladder is bustling with activity, herring in the hundreds fighting their way up the ladder to the reservoir to spawn. Likewise, there is much human activity, as anglers fill up their bait buckets. Back on the river, you will be traveling with the current. Notice the influence of fresh water here; the yellow flowers of jewelweed light up the edges of the river. Swamp azaleas along the banks, abloom in summer, fill the air with a sweet aroma. The bright red flower on the water's edge is cardinal flower, a rare find on the Cape today. Take a short detour south through the cattail marsh as it winds its way inland. As you make your way along the twisting creek, watch for swans and their huge nests, built amid the cattails. Reverse and paddle back to the Herring River channel and continue traveling with the outgoing tide.

The river will wind through a cattail marsh. At the second bridge, a footbridge, pass under it and take out on the left side. This footbridge is accessible from North Road. If you plan to continue your trip to the MA 28 launch and make this a one-way trip (and you have spotted a vehicle there), follow the gently flowing river as the brackish water turns to salt and salt-marsh plants dominate the riverscape. Along the way, detour from the river and explore some of the small feeder creeks.

23. *Quivett Creek, Brewster*

Maps:
> USGS Harwich Quadrangle
> USGS Dennis Quadrangle

Launch location: The end of Paines Creek Road, Brewster

Habitats: Salt marsh, tidal creek

Length of trip: 4 hours

Type of trip: Round-trip paddle with stops on a marsh and Wing Island

Paddling distance: 5 miles

Paddling conditions: Flat water on creek, swells and wind possible on bay

Current: Flood in/ebb out. Tide turns in marsh 2 hours after launch.

Launch time: On high, 1 hour before Boston high

Permits, fees, parking: Very limited, town sticker required

Facilities: None

Handicap access: Sandy beach

Directions to launch: From US 6, take exit 9, and follow MA 134 north to MA 6A. Go right and follow MA 6A east for 2.75 miles, then bear left at a fork onto Lower Road. Drive 0.2 mile and turn left onto Paines Creek Road, then go 0.7 mile to the launch.

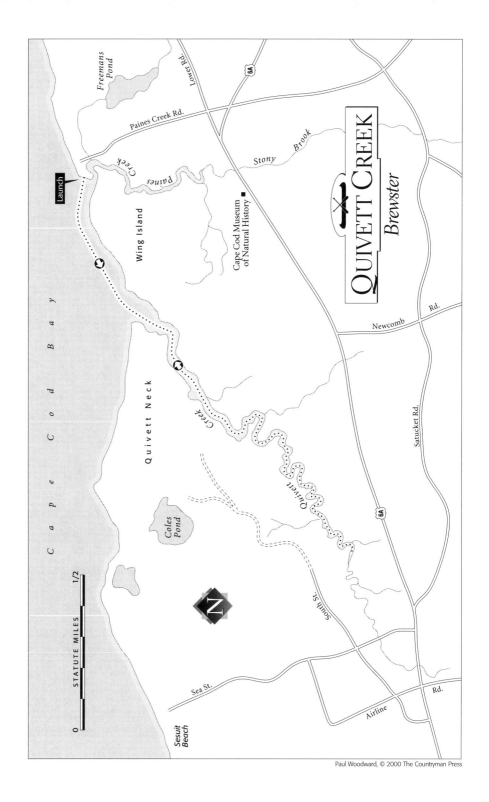

QUIVETT CREEK
Brewster

Launch

Cape Cod Museum
of Natural History ■

Freemans Pond

Lower Rd.

6A

Paines Creek Rd.

Stony Brook

Paines Creek

Wing Island

Cape Cod Bay

Quivett Neck

Quivett Creek

Coles Pond

Newcomb Rd.

Satucket Rd.

6A

South St.

Sea St.

Sesuit Beach

Airline Rd.

STATUTE MILES

0   1/2

*Double-crested cormorants often stand in
this pose to dry their wings.*

The Tour

Quivett Creek, located on Cape Cod Bay, serves as a boundary line between Dennis and Brewster. It runs along the west side of Wing Island. The Native Americans called it Shuckquan, from the Algonquian word *sequanamanquock,* meaning "spring or early-summer fish."

Together with its sister creek, Paines, which lies on the east side of Wing Island, Quivett is the site of the premier herring run on the Cape. Each spring, herring by the hundreds come in from Cape Cod Bay, swim into Paines and Quivett Creeks, then through the numerous marsh tributaries and into Stony Brook, climb the stone fish ladder at the Grist Mill, and enter the freshwater ponds (Lower Mill, Upper Mill, and Walkers), where they spawn.

Since 1995, Wing Island has been the site of an archaeological program under the direction of the Cape Cod Museum of Natural History. Surrounded on three sides by the marshes of Quivett and Paines Creeks, Wing Island was a bountiful area for the Native Americans who lived there. The island provided shelter for their garden plots and wig-wams, and the salt marshes and tidal flats provided an abundant supply of food and raw materials.

A unique feature of Quivett Creek, if you are able to get to it, is that you will have it all to yourself. It is only 1½ miles long but seems like at least twice that as the creek meanders on and on. It is well protected from wind and waves by the surrounding marsh and upland areas. However, access is another matter. There is a small parking lot at the end of Paines Creek Road, but go early because there is space for only ten cars. You'll also need a town of Brewster parking sticker (see Resource Appendix).

The first leg of the tour will put you out into Cape Cod Bay. Keep Wing Island to your left and head west for ½ mile until you reach the mouth of Quivett Creek. Once in the creek, the trip is a leisurely paddle through the marsh. You can explore side creeks or just stay in the main channel until it ends at MA 6A.

When the tide begins to ebb, start back. Coming out of the marsh, you will be in a rip current that will carry you out into the bay. It is best to ferry (sideslip) across the current. If you delay for too long in the marsh, you will be faced with the tidal flats that extend for 1¼ miles off-shore at low tide. Once out of Quivett Creek, keep Wing Island to your right as you paddle back to Paines Creek. You may want to stop on Wing Island and take a walk up to the bluff, which provides a beautiful, panoramic view of Cape Cod Bay.

24. *Upper and Lower Mill Ponds, Brewster*

Maps:
 USGS Harwich Quadrangle
 USGS Dennis Quadrangle
Launch location: Punkhorn Conservation Lands, Brewster
Habitats: Freshwater kettle pond bordered by conservation land
Length of trip: As long as you want to make it, or at least 2 hours
Type of trip: Round-trip paddle and walk
Paddling distance: 4 miles
Paddling conditions: Flat water on open pond

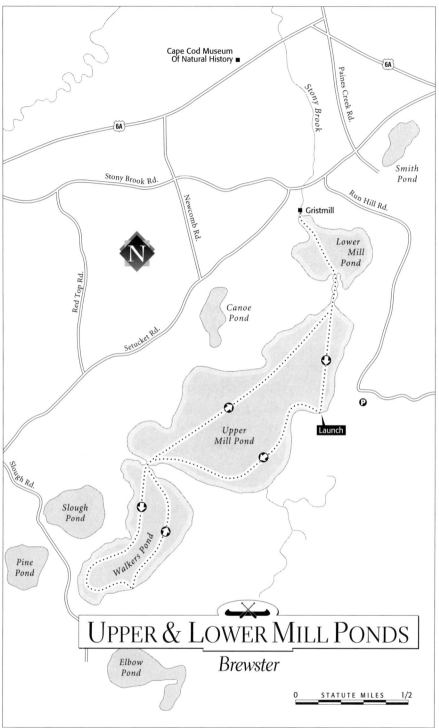

Cape Cod Museum
Of Natural History ■

6A

Stony Brook

Paines Creek Rd.

6A

Stony Brook Rd.

Newcomb Rd.

Run Hill Rd.

Smith
Pond

■ Gristmill

Lower
Mill
Pond

Red Top Rd.

Canoe
Pond

Setucket Rd.

P

Upper
Mill Pond

Launch

Slough Rd.

Slough
Pond

Walkers Pond

Pine
Pond

UPPER & LOWER MILL PONDS

Brewster

Elbow
Pond

0   STATUTE MILES   1/2

Paul Woodward, © 2000 The Countryman Press

Current: None
Launch time: Anytime
Permits, fees, parking: No permits or fees required to park or
    launch. Medium-sized, gravel parking lot.
Facilities: Portable toilet
Handicap access: Paved ramp
Directions to launch: From US 6, take exit 10, and follow MA 124
    north to MA 6A. Turn left onto MA 6A west, drive 1.8 miles, and
    bear left onto Stony Brook Road. In 0.6 mile turn left onto Run
    Hill Road, then go 1.3 miles to the Punkhorn Conservation
    Lands parking lot.

The Ponds

Upper and Lower Mill Ponds are freshwater kettle-hole ponds, joined
by the "narrows," a shallow passage adorned with rose bushes. Cape
Cod has more than 500 fresh- and saltwater kettle ponds; their average
size is 90 acres and average depth is 65 feet. What all these ponds have in
common is how they were formed: As the glaciers receded more than
12,000 years ago, ice blocks melted and left behind holes with kettle-
shaped, rounded bottoms.

The Grist Mill at Lower Mill Pond in Brewster

The Mill Ponds abound in natural beauty and are very paddler-friendly; no gasoline-powered boats or jet skis are allowed on the pond. From the launch, you begin your paddle on Upper Mill Pond. Follow the shore west and pass through a small clearing into Walkers Pond and paddle along the shore. Observe Eastern painted turtles sunning themselves on fallen branches and the many freshwater plants in seasonal bloom. White and yellow water lilies are often blooming along shallow edges of the pond, with dragonflies and damselflies darting from pad to pad. The scent of swamp azalea drifts across the water from the white flowering bushes lining the shore.

Circumnavigate Walker's Pond and make a stop, south of the town landing, at the clearing on the hill. Walkers Pond and Upper Mill Pond are bordered by the Punkhorn Parklands, an 800-acre conservation area purchased by the town of Brewster between 1985 and 1987. There are 5 miles of trails through, and around, freshwater marshes, kettle-hole ponds, abandoned cranberry bogs, and wooded forest. Take time to explore. The signboard in the parking lot shows trail routes and will give you a good sense of the layout of the area.

Back on the water, paddle across Upper Mill Pond, heading east to Lower Mill Pond. You will see the narrows coming into view, and when there you may have to walk your boat a short distance if the water level is low. If you are paddling a kayak, you may want to break down your paddle so you have one blade to propel yourself forward through this confined passage. In summer, swamp roses flourish, attracting many bumblebees, and sweet pepper bush fills the air with its pungent sweet aroma. Paddle across the pond to the Stony Brook Grist Mill. The mill was built in 1873 and is one of the oldest water-driven mills on the Cape. You can tie up at the wall, hoist yourself up, and take a tour of the mill to watch grain being ground. It is open to the public in the summer on Friday from 2 to 5 PM. In spring a tremendous amount of activity accompanies the herring run, when the herring swim up from Cape Cod Bay into Paines and Quivett Creeks, then into Stony Brook, and up the natural rock fish ladder into both Mill Ponds to spawn. There are rest rooms and a picnic table at the mill.

Eastern painted turtles bask among pickerelweed and water willow.

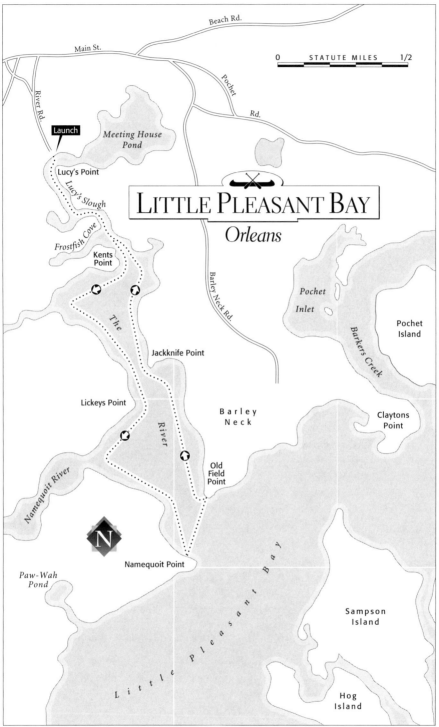

Beach Rd.

Main St.

Pochet

River Rd.

Rd.

Launch

Meeting House
Pond

Lucy's Point

Lucy's Slough

Frostfish Cove

Kents
Point

The

Jackknife Point

Lickeys Point

River

Namequoit River

Old
Field
Point

Barley Neck Rd.

Pochet
Inlet

Barkers Creek

Pochet
Island

B A R L E Y
N E C K

Claytons
Point

N

Namequoit Point

Paw-Wah
Pond

L i t t l e   P l e a s a n t   B a y

Sampson
Island

Hog
Island

0   STATUTE MILES   1/2

LITTLE PLEASANT BAY
Orleans

PART IV

Lower Cape Paddling Tours

25. Little Pleasant Bay, Orleans

Maps:
    USGS Orleans Quadrangle
    USGS Chatham Quadrangle

Launch location: River Road Landing, Orleans

Habitats: Bay, tidal river, island, salt marsh

Length of trip: 3 hours

Type of trip: Round-trip paddle with a stop on Namequoit Point for a swim

Paddling distance: 3 miles

Paddling conditions: Tidal river and bay

Current: Ebb out/flood in. Tide turns at Namequoit Point 1 hour 30 minutes after launch.

Launch time: On low, 1 hour 45 minutes after Boston low

Permits, fees, parking: No permits or fees required to park or launch. Small lot with on-street parking.

Facilities: None

Handicap access: Paved ramps

Directions to launch: From US 6, take exit 12 onto MA 6A north. Turn right onto Eldredge Parkway, drive 1 mile, and turn right onto Main Street. After 0.3 mile turn right onto River Road, and drive 0.4 mile to the town landing.

The Tour

Little Pleasant Bay is a fitting name, as many a paddler, sailor, angler, or sunbather will attest to. Little Pleasant is part of Pleasant Bay, the largest bay on the southern side of the Cape, which shares its waters with Orleans, Chatham, Harwich, and Brewster. Little Pleasant Bay embodies less than half of Pleasant Bay, with Nauset Beach and the Cape Cod National Seashore to the east providing shelter to Sampson Island and Hog Island and creating a healthy and productive estuary.

The salt ponds in this area are mixed with fresh water fed by springs and seepage. To the north is Meeting House Pond, and on the western shore are Kescayogansett (or Lonnie's), Areys, and Paw Wah Ponds. The bay is rich in Native American history, with many of the poetic Indian names still in use today, though somewhat anglicized. Until the 18th century, the bay was known by its Indian name, *Monomoyick*, later translated by white settlers to The Great Bay.

To the south are Sipson and Little Sipson Islands, where the narrows generate a quick current into "Great" Pleasant Bay, best navigated by experienced paddlers. However, several good options present themselves from this launch site.

Launch from River Road Landing and you will be on what is now known as simply The River. In earlier times it was called Eel River and Higgin's River. It is a good place to begin your tour of the bay. Located at the landing on River Road is a little gingerbread-style building, in disrepair, with a historical marker denoting it the ancient POCHET POND PACKET LANDING for passengers and freight traveling to and arriving from New York City. From the launch, swing around to your left to enter Meeting House Pond, which you can explore before you begin your paddle down The River and into the bay. This saltwater pond is only about ¼ mile across at its widest, but it's a good place to paddle around and look at all the boats at anchor.

About ½ mile downriver from the launch, on the eastern side, is a marsh inlet known as Lucy's Slough. Paddle into this marshy area and keep your eyes open, scanning underwater for red encrusting bryozoans that are really orange and have the appearance of delicate lacework,

Launching at the historic Pochet Pond Packet Landing

*Late afternoon can be an especially
magical time to be on the water.*

growing on stones that were once the foundation of an old tide-powered grain mill. Another brilliant animal to look for in these shallow waters is red beard sponge, one of the most common and easily recognizable sponges on the Cape. Paddle back out into what is known as Lucy's Crotch to return to The River. The first inlet on the western shore is Frostfish Cove, and the next Kescayogansett Pond. Farther south is the Namequoit River that enters Areys Pond. If you decide to explore any of these inlets, expect a hard paddle in against the outgoing tide but an easy paddle on the way back out to The River.

The channel to Kescayogansett Pond is not very long and has some interesting natural and cultural history. Look at the bank on the northern side, near the boulders in the water, and you will see fresh water trickling down the bank from a spring. Look for holes in the bank where red fox make their home. Across the pond is a herring run that flows out of Pilgrim Lake.

Back on the river, our final destination is Namequoit Point on the western shore, easily identifiable by the sandbar and converging waves. Take a break here. The tide should have turned by now, allowing for an easy paddle back to the launch.

26. *Sampson Island and Broad Creek, Orleans*

Maps:
> USGS Orleans Quadrangle
> USGS Chatham Quadrangle

Launch location: Portanimicut Road, Orleans

Habitats: Bay, tidal river, island, salt marsh

Length of trip: 4 hours

Type of trip: Round-trip paddle with time to explore Sampson Island

Paddling distance: 5 miles

Paddling conditions: Open bay, against tide first 1½ miles

Current: Flood in/ebb out. Tide turns at northern end of Sampson Island 2 hours 30 minutes after launch.

Launch time: On high, same as Boston high

Permits, fees, parking: No permits or fees required to park or launch. Small, paved lot and on-street parking.

Facilities: None

Handicap access: Paved ramp

Directions to launch: From US 6, take exit 12 to MA 6A north. Turn right onto Eldredge Parkway, drive 0.8 mile, and turn right onto MA 28 south. Drive along MA 28 for 2.5 miles and then bear left onto Quanset Road. After 0.1 mile bear left onto Portanimicut Road; follow it 1 mile to the landing.

The Tour

Launch from Portanimicut Road, and before entering the bay, paddle into Paw-Wah Pond and make an offering to the Paw-Wah Medicine Man. As legend has it, one winter he moved his wigwam onto the ice to fish, fell through, and was never seen again. To have any luck when

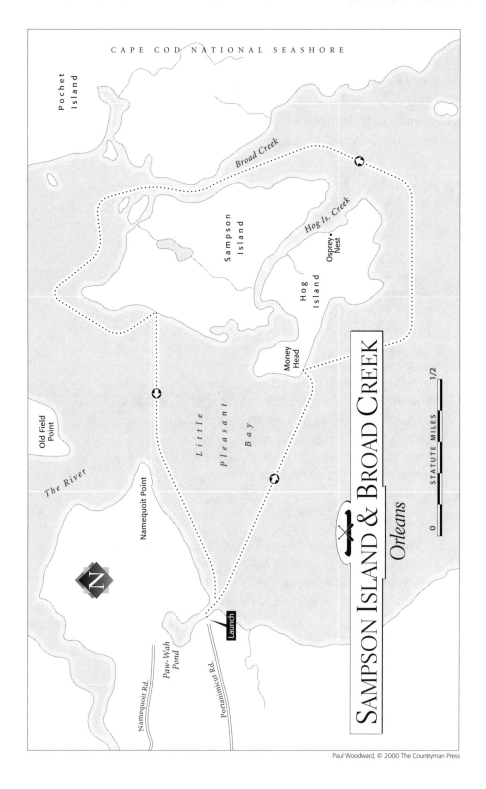

CAPE COD NATIONAL SEASHORE

Pochet Island

Broad Creek

Sampson Island

Hog Is. Creek

Osprey Nest

Hog Island

Money Head

Old Field Point

The River

Little Pleasant Bay

Namequoit Point

N

Launch

Paw-Wah Pond

Namequoit Rd.

Portanimicut Rd.

SAMPSON ISLAND & BROAD CREEK

Orleans

0   STATUTE MILES   1/2

Paul Woodward, © 2000 The Countryman Press

fishing in the pond, you must drop in a few quid of tobacco as a peace offering. Perhaps that holds true with the wind as well—make an offering, and you will have calm waters.

From the pond, paddle into the bay, past glacial erratics. The first huge rock is known as Seal Rock, where seals are spotted in the winter months. Dead ahead, across the bay, are Sampson and Hog Islands. Hog Island is on the southern side of Sampson, bounding the entrance to Broad Creek. Both Sampson and Hog Islands are privately owned, but the owners allow visitors (but no camping or campfires). Sampson Island was named for a chief of the Nauset Indians, Hog Island for the livestock that once grazed there. Take a rest break on Money Head, the northern tip of Hog Island. Perhaps look for treasures; legend has it that Captain Kidd buried his unlawful gains here when the British were in hot pursuit. You may not find anything of monetary value, but the island holds many nonmonetary gems for the beachcomber.

As you leave Money Head, keep an easterly tack; you will see Nauset Beach (part of the Cape Cod National Seashore) in the distance. Swing around Hog Island and head north, past Hog Island Creek, where a pair of osprey reside on the northern shore of the is-

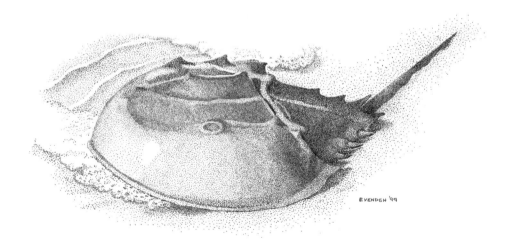

The prehistoric-looking horseshoe crab dwells along the shore.

land. Watch the sky for these skillful fish hawks as they hunt for prey and return to their nest with fresh fish to feed their young. Paddle through tranquil Broad Creek, with Nauset Beach providing shelter from the breaking waves of the Atlantic Ocean. Round the northern tip of Sampson Island; take a rest break on the sandy shore. Walk along the beach and notice the banks, where in a couple of places erosion has revealed Indian middens (refuse heaps of old shells), a visual and tangible link to the past.

By now, the tide will have turned, and you will have an outgoing tide for the journey back across the bay to the launch.

27. *Pochet Inlet, Orleans*

Maps:
> USGS Orleans Quadrangle
> USGS Chatham Quadrangle

Launch location: Portanimicut Road, Orleans

Habitats: Bay, tidal river, island, salt marsh

Length of trip: 5 hours

Type of trip: Round-trip paddle with a stop on Sampson Island

Paddling distance: 6 miles

Paddling conditions: Open bay, tidal creeks

Current: Flood in/ebb out. Tide turns at Pochet Inlet 2 hours 45 minutes after launch.

Launch time: On high, 45 minutes after Boston high

Permits, fees, parking: No permits or fees required to park or launch. Small, paved lot and on-street parking.

Facilities: None

Handicap access: Paved ramp

Directions to launch: From US 6, take exit 12 to MA 6A north. Go right onto Eldredge Parkway, drive 0.8 mile, and turn right onto MA 28 north. Drive along MA 28 for 2.5 miles and bear left onto Quanset Road. After 0.1 mile bear left onto Portanimicut Road; follow it 1 mile to the landing.

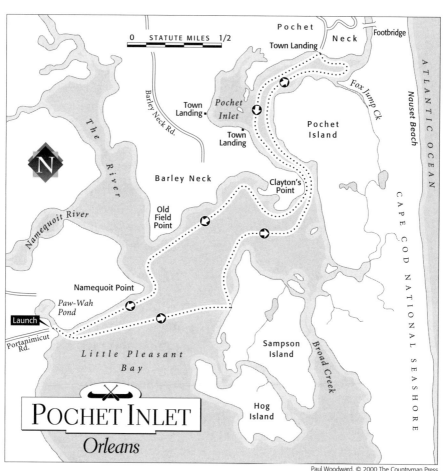

The Tour

This trip into Pochet Inlet is closely related to the Sampson Island tour (see Tour 26) and yet deserves a separate outing all of its own.

Launch from Portanimicut Road and paddle into the bay, following a northeast heading for Sampson Island. Near the island, the eelgrass is so dense in places that you may snag your paddle in it. These ribbonlike, slender blades of grass are not a seaweed, but a true flowering plant with stems and roots. Eelgrass provides scallops, clams, crabs, and many other marine organisms a place to anchor, seek shelter, and reproduce. Take a break on Sampson Island and observe the diversity of marine life scurrying about your boat. This clean and productive bay harbors an abundance of clams, snails, and crabs. Watch as green crabs scuttle about in their sidestepping manner. If you feel a pinch on your toe, it is no doubt a lady crab. Observe little hermit crabs, in constant competition for a new shell to occupy once they have outgrown their present one.

After launching from Sampson Island, resume your trip northeast to Pochet Inlet, staying clear of the aquaculture nets, marked with orange ball floats. These nets belong to shellfish farmers who are growing clams and scallops. Paddle up Barker's Creek into Pochet Inlet and then up into Pochet Creek, passing under the footbridge that provides access to Nauset Beach. The creek goes through salt marshes and then dead-ends. It will be tight quarters for turning. There are a number of town landings in the inlet where you can stop for a rest break before paddling back to the launch at Portanimicut.

28. *Stage Harbor, Chatham*

Maps:
> USGS Chatham Quadrangle
Launch location: Vineyard Avenue, Chatham
Habitats: Tidal river, open harbor, barrier beach
Length of trip: 4 hours
Type of trip: Round-trip paddle and walk
Paddling distance: 5 miles
Paddling conditions: Flat water on protected river into open harbor

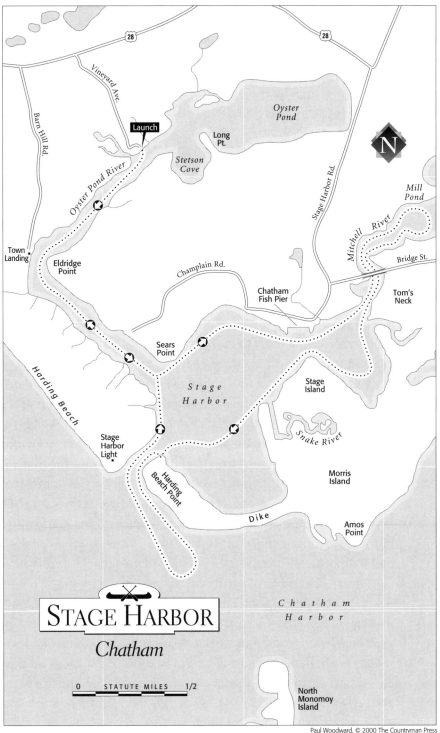

N

28
28

Vineyard Ave.

Oyster
Pond

Launch

Barn Hill Rd.

Long
Pt.

Stetson
Cove

Mill
Pond

Oyster Pond River

Stage Harbor Rd.

Mitchell River

Town
Landing

Eldridge
Point

Champlain Rd.

Bridge St.

Tom's
Neck

Chatham
Fish Pier

Sears
Point

Harding Beach

Stage
Island

Stage
Harbor

Stage
Harbor
Light

Snake River

Harding
Beach Point

Morris
Island

Dike

Amos
Point

STAGE HARBOR

Chatham

Chatham
Harbor

0   STATUTE MILES   1/2

North
Monomoy
Island

Paul Woodward, © 2000 The Countryman Press

Current: Ebb out/flood in. Tide turns at Harding Beach 2½ hours
  after launch.
Launch time: On low, 1½ hour before Boston low
Permits, fees, parking: No permits or fees required to park or
  launch. Small, dirt lot.
Facilities: None
Handicap access: Launch from sandy shore
Directions to launch: From US 6, take exit 11, and follow MA 137
  south to MA 28. Turn left onto MA 28 south, drive 1.9 miles,
  and turn right onto Vineyard Avenue. Drive 0.4 mile to the town
  landing.

The Tour

Vineyard Avenue town landing has a dirt parking lot and dirt launch.
The lot is small and used by commercial clammers who keep their boats
anchored here and ready to go. Be courteous and don't block their access, for once the tide has turned, they don't want to be delayed.

Oyster Pond River, a tidal river flowing in and out of Oyster Pond,
is a scenic, busy inlet with many fishing and pleasure boats coming and
going. Stay off to the side, as the channel is rather narrow with boats
tied up at floating docks. Paddle downriver past another town landing
on Barn Hill Road, and out around Eldridge Point. When the river enters Stage Harbor, head north over shallow eelgrass beds. If the wind
and current aren't too strong, enter the Mitchell River leading into Mill
Pond. Passing under Bridge Street may be tough with an outgoing tide,
but it is worth the effort. Once in little Mill Pond you will have a
panoramic view of a quaint New England village with gentle hills,
church steeples, and an old gristmill dating from the 1800s.

At low tide, many shorebirds will be feeding on the exposed mud-
flats and marsh. The easiest to identify are the herons and egrets. The
great blue heron, bluish gray with a yellow beak, is the largest of these
wading birds, standing 3 to 4 feet tall. The snowy egret and great egret
are both white; however, the snowy egret is almost half the size of the
great egret and has a black beak, black legs, and bright yellow feet. The
great egret also has black legs but black feet and a yellow beak. If you

Stage Harbor Light, Chatham

see them in a pensive pose, stop and watch how these beautiful birds so gracefully stalk their prey.

Paddle back out into Stage Harbor. On the southeast side of the harbor is Morris Island, extended by a barrier beach locally called the dike. At low tide on the exposed sandflats you will see many clammers digging for quahogs or steamer clams with a rake or a plunger (a pole with a rubber piece on the end resembling a household drain plunger).

With the outgoing tide and a favorable wind, paddle beyond the dike and stop on the sandflats that fringe the northern tip of North Monomoy Island. Out on the flats you will see an array of shorebirds, so keep your field guide handy to help identify the many different species of terns and sandpipers. With binoculars, you can clearly see the Monomoy Islands, which were separated from Morris Island by a storm in 1958. They became North Monomoy and South Monomoy in 1978 when a northeast blizzard caused a breach. Most of Monomoy was designated a Wilderness Area in 1970 and is known as the Monomoy National Wildlife Refuge, managed by the U.S. Fish and Wildlife Service.

Be on the alert for changes in weather. Fog is prevalent in warmer months and can move in very quickly and reduce visibility to zero.

When you see the tidal flow begin to change, paddle back and make a stop on Harding Beach, where you will see the Stage Harbor Light, now privately owned. Take a walk on the beach and do some beach-combing along Nantucket Sound. With the incoming tide, it will be an easy paddle back to the launch.

29. *Nauset Marsh, Eastham*

Maps:
> USGS Orleans Quadrangle

Launch location: Hemenway Road, Eastham

Habitats: Salt pond bay, saltwater marsh, sandflats, barrier beach

Length of trip: 4 hours

Type of trip: Round-trip paddle and walk

Paddling distances:
> Cedar Bank, 4 miles
> Inlet Marsh, 6 miles
> Nauset Beach, 4 miles

Paddling conditions:
> Cedar Bank, flat water on creek
> Inlet Marsh, flat water, quick current, sandbars
> Nauset Beach, tidal flats and loose barrier beach sand

Currents:
> Cedar Bank, flood in/ebb out. Tide turns in Nauset Bay approximately 1 hour 15 minutes after launch.
> Inlet Marsh, ebb out/flood in. Tide turns at Inlet Marsh 1 hour 45 minutes after launch.
> Nauset Beach, ebb out/flood in. Tide turns at Nauset Beach 2 hours after launch.

Launch times:
> Cedar Bank, on high, 30 minutes after Boston high
> Inlet Marsh, on low, 1 hour 15 minutes after Boston low
> Nauset Beach, on low, 30 minutes after Boston low

Permits, fees, parking: Permit required; check with town hall.

Facilities: Rest rooms located nearby at entrance to National Seashore's Fort Hill Trail

Handicap access: Paved ramp

> **Directions to launch:** From Orleans rotary, take US 6 north, go 1.8 miles and turn right onto Hemenway Road. After 0.3 mile you'll come to the town landing. From US 6 south, drive 1.1 miles past the entrance to National Seashore Visitor Center, turn left onto Hemenway Road, and continue to the town landing.

The Tours

Nauset Marsh, located within the confines of the Cape Cod National Seashore, is an extensive low marsh that is washed twice a day by the tides. The marsh was formed when sand drifting southward created a barrier beach almost entirely across the mouth of Salt Pond Bay, with but one inlet to let the flow of the tides from the Atlantic Ocean into Nauset Harbor and the surrounding marsh. This obstruction has created one of nature's most productive ecosystems, swarming with marine life. An array of microscopic organisms provide food for the many creatures, such as shellfish and open-ocean fish, that use the shallow, protected salt marsh as a nursery. The barrier beach is a haven for colonies of common, least, and roseate terns.

There are many little creeks, bays, and tidal pools to explore on Nauset Marsh; paddling to most is dependent on a favorable tide. We've combined three of our favorites in this section, which can be combined or taken as separate outings.

Cedar Bank Creek

Along the northern border of Nauset Marsh lies Cedar Bank Creek, aptly named for the red cedars along the shore. A launch on an incoming tide into Salt Pond Bay will allow you to float past the entrance to Salt Pond (where the visitors center at the National Seashore is located) and into Cedar Bank Creek. The creek will provide plenty of water for paddling, but you need only wander into the marsh to find shallows. Look for sand collars, the egg case of a moon snail, on the flats. Moon snails are ferocious feeders, boring their way through the shells of bivalves and other snails.

Return to the creek for an easy paddle to Nauset Bay. The structure looming overhead is the Nauset Coast Guard Station. The beach below the station is a good place to stop for a break. From here you can walk across the beach to the Atlantic Ocean side and do some beachcombing or watch the breakers coming ashore. After days of stormy weather, you can hear the thunderous waves pounding the shore from the shelter of Nauset Marsh.

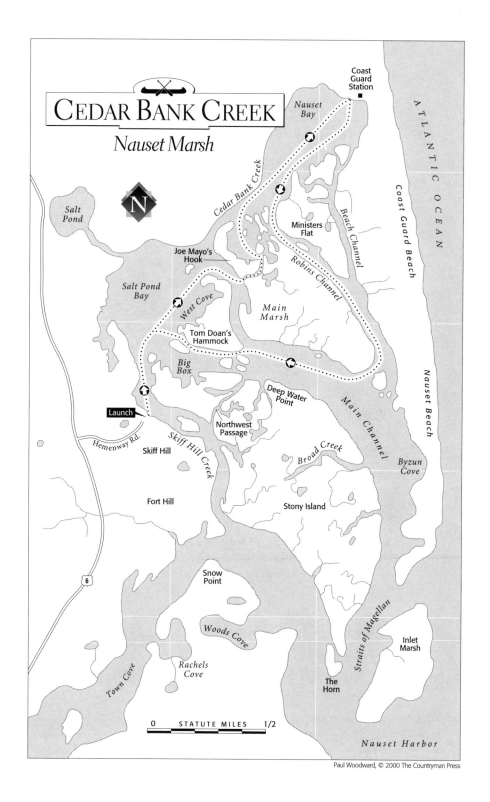

CEDAR BANK CREEK

Nauset Marsh

N

Coast Guard Station

Nauset Bay

ATLANTIC OCEAN

Coast Guard Beach

Salt Pond

Cedar Bank Creek

Ministers Flat

Beach Channel

Joe Mayo's Hook

Robins Channel

Salt Pond Bay

West Cove

Main Marsh

Tom Doan's Hammock

Big Box

Deep Water Point

Launch

Northwest Passage

Main Channel

Skiff Hill Creek

Hemenway Rd.

Skiff Hill

Broad Creek

Byzun Cove

Nauset Beach

Fort Hill

Stony Island

6

Snow Point

Straits of Magellan

Inlet Marsh

Woods Cove

Rachels Cove

The Horn

Town Cove

0   STATUTE MILES   1/2

Nauset Harbor

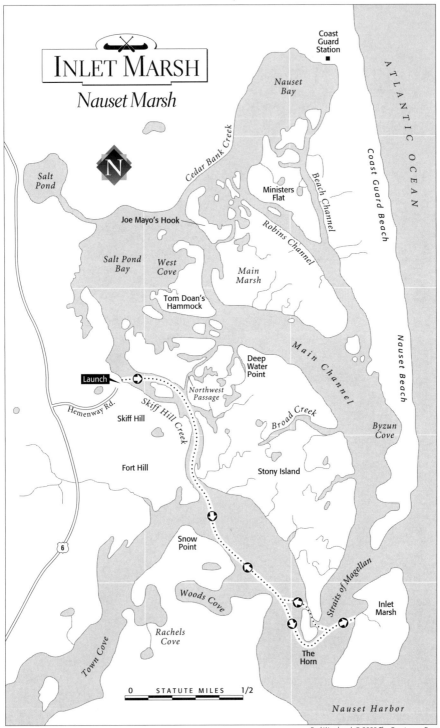

INLET MARSH

Nauset Marsh

Salt
Pond

N

Coast
Guard
Station

Nauset
Bay

ATLANTIC OCEAN

Cedar Bank Creek

Joe Mayo's Hook

Ministers
Flat

Beach Channel

Coast Guard Beach

Salt Pond
Bay

West
Cove

Main
Marsh

Robins Channel

Tom Doan's
Hammock

Deep
Water
Point

Northwest
Passage

Main Channel

Launch

Hemenway Rd.

Skiff Hill Creek

Skiff Hill

Broad Creek

Byzun
Cove

Nauset Beach

Fort Hill

Stony Island

6

Snow
Point

Woods Cove

Straits of Magellan

Inlet
Marsh

Rachels
Cove

The
Horn

Town Cove

0   STATUTE MILES   1/2

Nauset Harbor

When the tide turns, head back down through Cedar Bank Creek, or try Beach or Robins Channels, past Ministers Flat, where hundreds of shorebirds congregate on the exposed sandflats to feed. Swing around Main Marsh and into Main Channel, where the water is crystal clear, providing a lucent underwater view of striped bass passing under your boat's hull. Upon the rich brown peat banks, brilliant orange sea stars and male fiddler crabs, with their huge cream-colored claw, create a colorful contrast. Paddle through Big Box and back to the landing. All of these creeks can be somewhat indistinguishable at high tide; however, when the tide drops, a maze of channels appears. If you follow the sun as it sets in the west, you will never get lost on your return route.

Inlet Marsh

The Inlet Marsh route is the "birdwatcher's route." On an outgoing tide, paddle south through Skiff Hill Creek. On the inland shore, high on Fort Hill, is the best location for spectacular views of Nauset Marsh, Nauset Spit, and the Atlantic Ocean. The Fort Hill Trail is also one of the best trails for birders hoping to catch a glimpse of black-crowned night-herons and great blue herons.

The entrance to Town Cove will be on your right, but continue on course into Nauset Harbor. Inlet Marsh, in the center of the harbor, is a great place to stop. During spring and summer, this small island and marsh is home to colonies of terns and laughing gulls. The terns nest on the north side and the gulls on the south side. The upland is off-limits to visitors, but you can either walk or paddle around the marsh and observe the frenzied behavior of these territorial birds. Be on the lookout for the occasional intrepid tern that thinks your head would make an excellent spot to relieve itself, in hopes of sending you on your way.

After the tide turns, paddle around the Horn or through the Straits of Magellan and back up Skiff Hill Creek to the landing. Make it a slow paddle back, or you may get stuck on the sandflats and have to wait for higher water to get you off.

Nauset Beach via Main Channel

This low-tide trip begins with a paddle through the Northwest Passage and a stop at Deep Water Point. The expansive sandflats, exposed at this tide, make for an interesting walk. Try to spot a water spout from a clam burrowed below the surface, filtering detritus and shooting water up from its siphon as you approach. If you notice a keyhole-shaped opening in the sand, it is likely made by a common razor clam. Some are as long as 10 inches, and they anchor tenaciously in the wet sand, making all your efforts to extract the animal futile. Imagine what this area looks like at high tide, submerged beneath 6 feet of water, leaving but a few distinguishable channels.

Continue south down the Main Channel and take out at Byzun Cove for a walk on Nauset Beach, which hosts the largest tern colony in New England. Obey any signs and roped-off areas during nesting season and do not venture into the tern territory. In spring the place is swarming with common terns (the most prevalent), roseate terns, and least terns, both on the federal list of threatened species. Common terns are fearless defenders of their nest and have been known to dive and peck at a human's head to keep the intruder away.

When the tide turns, head back to the landing via the Main Channel. Don't be surprised to see buoys marking lobster traps. Lobsters are generally thought of as living in rocky ledges along Maine's coast, but here in Nauset Marsh, small 1½- to 2-pound female lobsters burrow into the peat banks, where they lay their eggs. Look for the holes, about 4 inches in diameter, and you may spot a lobster.

Buffleheads

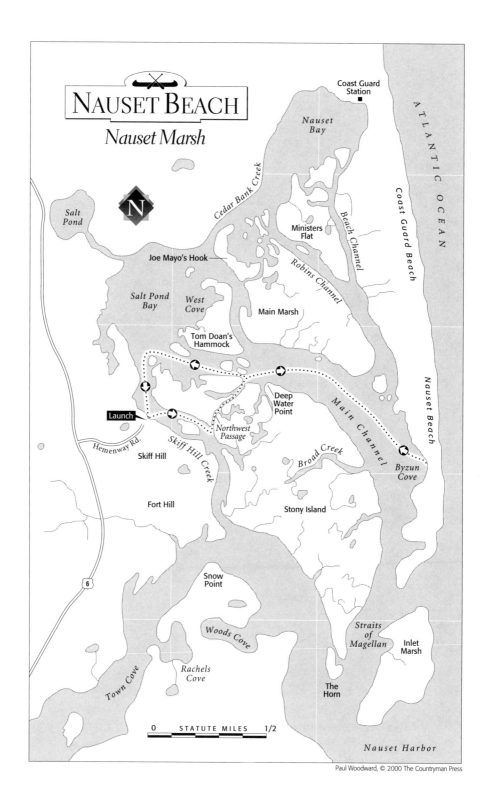

NAUSET BEACH
Nauset Marsh

N

Salt Pond

Cedar Bank Creek

Coast Guard Station

Nauset Bay

ATLANTIC OCEAN

Coast Guard Beach

Ministers Flat

Beach Channel

Joe Mayo's Hook

Robins Channel

Salt Pond Bay

West Cove

Main Marsh

Tom Doan's Hammock

Deep Water Point

Main Channel

Launch

Northwest Passage

Nauset Beach

Hemenway Rd.

Skiff Hill Creek

Skiff Hill

Broad Creek

Byzun Cove

Fort Hill

Stony Island

6

Snow Point

Woods Cove

Straits of Magellan

Inlet Marsh

Rachels Cove

Town Cove

The Horn

0   STATUTE MILES   1/2

Nauset Harbor

Paul Woodward, © 2000 The Countryman Press

A feeding frenzy of common terns,
who dive for small fish.

30. *Boat Meadow River, Eastham*

Maps:
>   USGS Orleans Quadrangle

Launch location: Bayview Road Landing, Eastham

Habitats: Salt marsh, brackish bog

Length of trip: 3½ hours

Type of trip: Round-trip paddle

Paddling distance: 4 miles

Paddling conditions: Flat water in protected marsh

Current: Flood in/ebb out. Tide turns in Boat Meadow Bog 1 hour 45 minutes after launch.

Launch time: On high, 30 minutes before Boston high

Permits, fees, parking: No permits or fees required to launch. Dirt parking lot.

Facilities: None

Handicap access: Access to water via sandy beach

Directions to launch: From US 6, take the Rock Harbor exit off the Orleans rotary, turn left, and follow the road for 0.3 mile. Turn right onto Bridge Road and continue 0.7 mile. At a fork bear left onto Bayview Road and continue to the parking lot.

The Tour

Once a major waterway, in the 17th century it would have been possible to navigate the Boat Meadow River from Cape Cod Bay, through Nauset Harbor, to the Atlantic Ocean. Today, this passage has been blocked by centuries of development, and in particular, the Orleans rotary. However, it is a beautiful, sheltered, easy paddle through salt marsh into a brackish bog.

Launch from the beach on an incoming tide, paddle around the boats at anchor, and head into the creek. You can either paddle up and around the little salt marsh island or take the shorter route into the main channel. Soon an impressive osprey nest on a pole platform will come into view. The platform, close to the edge of the marsh, offers an ideal view of these magnificent fish hawks. This is the first of two active osprey nests along the creek.

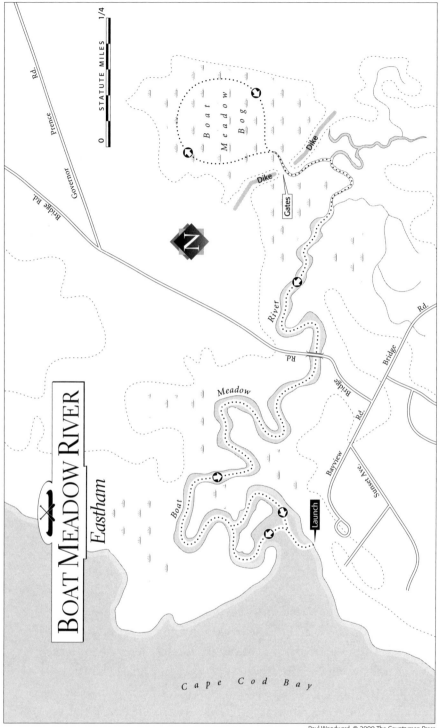

BOAT MEADOW RIVER
Eastham

Boat Meadow Bog

Dike

Dike

Gates

River

Meadow

Boat

Launch

Cape Cod Bay

Prence Rd.

Governor

Bridge Rd.

Rd.

Bridge

Bridge Rd.

Bayview

Sunset Ave.

STATUTE MILES
0   1/4

N

Paul Woodward, © 2000 The Countryman Press

*Stopping to talk things over in
Boat Meadow River.*

Continue on and you will pass under the Bridge Road bridge, rebuilt from a rustic wooden bridge to a modern-day cement and steel structure in 1999. Viewed from the river, it is quite wide, the current is slow, and there is sufficient headroom to pass underneath. With high water make a stop on the marsh for a break and a chance to observe the diverse plants that inhabit this productive ecosystem. The grass you see growing on the edge of the marsh is saltwater cordgrass *(Spartina alterniflora),* which grows from 1 to 8 feet tall; the low, velvet grass growing in mats away from the water's edge is salt hay grass *(Spartina patens).* Other species of plants colonizing the marsh are black rush and sea lavender. Of particular interest are the glassworts, with fleshy succulent stems that are bright green in summer and reddish green in autumn. Found in the sandy *pannes* (salty depressions), they are also known as sea pickles and make a tasty, salty garnish for salads.

Back on the creek, continue on the main channel, or detour and explore the other feeder creeks that all dead-end and can hold a surprise around the next bend. The main channel will narrow, and the current pick up as you approach the dike. You can paddle around the dike, which is no longer in operation. The gates have been removed, allowing salt water to pass into Boat Meadow Bog, which was once primarily fresh water but is now brackish. You can wander through a maze of little creeks, all of which eventually return to the bog lagoon, where, from the comfort of your boat, you can watch salt-marsh snails and mud snails feeding on algae on the cordgrass stems, or fiddler crabs burrowing in and out of the salt-marsh peat. Take the time to observe all the natural activity transpiring above and below your boat. Keep an eye on the grass under the water: It tells you which way the current is flowing. When the grass tells you the tide is flowing out, it is time to leave the bog and paddle back into the creek and return to the launch.

31. *Pamet River, Truro*

Maps:
> USGS Wellfleet Quadrangle

Launch locations:
> Pamet Village, Truro
> Depot Road, Pamet Harbor, Truro

Habitats: Freshwater areas, kettle-hole ponds

Length of trip: 3 hours

Type of trip: Round-trip paddle

Paddling distance: 4 miles

Paddling conditions: Slow water on narrow river; very shallow and mucky in areas

Current: Brackish fresh water; slight tidal influence. Water depth is dependent on rain and snow amounts.

Launch time: Anytime

Permits, fees, parking: No fees or permits required to launch. Off-road parking available across from launch.

Facilities: None

Handicap access: No ramp, launch via steep bank off road overpass

Directions to launch: To get to the culvert launch, from US 6 north take the exit for Pamet Village. Go right off the exit. Before stop sign, park on the grass on the side of the road. The launch is located across the road adjacent to the culvert.

> To get to the Pamet Harbor launch, from US 6 north take the exit for Pamet Village. At the end of the exit ramp, turn right onto South Pamet Road and go 0.1 mile. Take a left, then immediately bear right onto Depot Road. Follow Depot Road for 1.4 miles to the Pamet Harbor boat ramp.

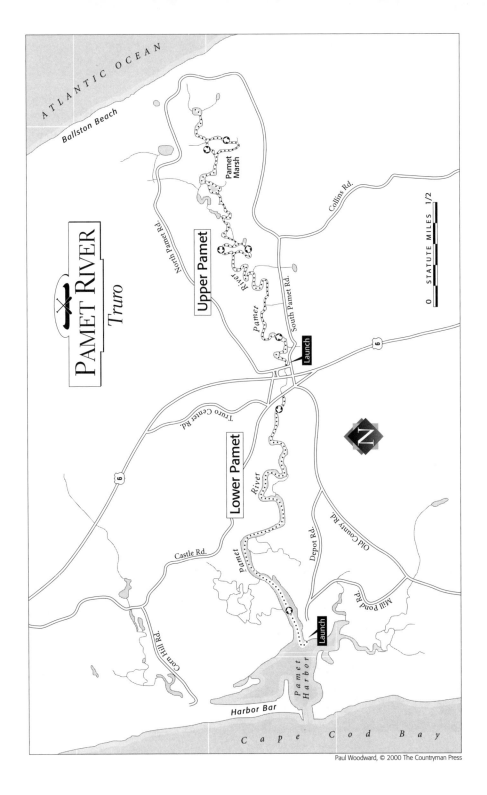

ATLANTIC OCEAN

Ballston Beach

PAMET RIVER
Truro

Pamet Marsh

Upper Pamet

North Pamet Rd.

Collins Rd.

Pamet River

South Pamet Rd.

Launch

6

Truro Center Rd.

Lower Pamet

Pamet River

N

6

Castle Rd.

Depot Rd.

Old County Rd.

Mill Pond Rd.

Corn Hill Rd.

Launch

Pamet Harbor

Harbor Bar

C a p e   C o d   B a y

0   STATUTE MILES   1/2

Paul Woodward, © 2000 The Countryman Press

The Tour

Just off the highway in Truro is the Pamet River. The mouth of the river is at Cape Cod Bay, and the Pamet meanders, almost, to the Atlantic Ocean. The Cape has but a few freshwater streams, their beds formed by glacial meltwater, as were kettle-hole ponds. Geologists refer to these outwash channels carved in glacial drift by melting blocks of ice as *pamets*. The river may also have been named for the Pamet Indians, a local tribe of the Algonquian Nation.

It is possible to launch from Pamet Harbor on an incoming tide and travel upriver for about a mile, but then you are faced with portaging over MA 6A and under US 6 in order to put in again along the culvert on South Pamet Road. Or, you can launch directly onto the freshwater portion and begin your journey. While this launch is a little difficult with a kayak more than 12 feet, a 16-foot canoe isn't a problem because of open access.

Once you leave the rumble of the highway behind and paddle down the valley, tranquility reins. A few houses are seen high on the hills, but as you paddle along, you are cloistered by trees and shrubs. Autumn is a particularly beautiful time on the river, the bright red

A typical "hogback" along the Pamet River.

Poison ivy helps stabilize the dunes—
be careful not to touch it!

berries of the common winterberry bush, a deciduous holly, providing a stunning accent to the green of the inkberry, grapevines, roses, and sweet pepper bushes. In the distance, white birches and pitch pines create an intercsting riverscape. Perhaps the most prolific and colorful vegetation in the autumn is furnished by the rich red leaves of the poison ivy growing along the banks and weaving its tendrils through the bushes and up the trunks of trees. On the surface of the water float mats of brilliant green duckweed, a source of food for the mallards and black ducks encountered here.

The river is dependent on rain and snow for its existence. In seasons of drought, the paddling becomes more of a poling exercise. There is an earthy scent of corn in the air, or perhaps it is the smell of the rich soil of this once-active farming community. About midway, the river forks; the left side is narrower with deeper water. Along the banks are a few clearings where you can stop and take an exploratory hike on the trails that border the river. (***Caution:*** Be sure to check your clothing and body for ticks.) Before you reach the end (or as far as you can go), the river will open, allowing you to see the panoramic backdrop of the Pamet Hills, known locally as "hogbacks," which are defined by *Webster's* as a "ridge with a sharp summit and steeply sloping sides." Beyond them lie Ballston Beach and the Atlantic Ocean.

The Pamet River is a nice change from saltwater paddling, it does not require you to coordinate with the tides, and it offers plenty of shelter on blustery days.

Resource Appendix

Contact the town offices and departments listed below for up-to-date information. Note that each town has its own fees, rules, and regulations governing beach parking and shellfishing, which are subject to change yearly.

If you will be shellfishing, it is recommended you contact the appropriate town office for their rules and regulations, where and when you may shellfish, and any areas that may be closed. There are no permits required for saltwater fishing. Freshwater fishing permits are: resident ($12.50); resident minor and senior ($6.50); nonresident ($11.50 for a 7-day permit).

Town of Barnstable, Hyannis (includes Centerville, Cotuit, Osterville)

Beach parking permits	508-790-6345	Resident: $15/vehicle Nonresident: $35/week/vehicle
Shellfish permits	508-790-6345	Resident: $20; senior: $6.50 Nonresident: $100
Recreation Department	508-862-4001	
Conservation Commission	508-862-4093	
Natural Resource Department	508-790-6272	
Harbormaster	508-790-6273	

Town of Bourne

Beach parking permits	508-759-0623	Resident: $15/vehicle Nonresident: $20/vehicle

Shellfish permits	508-759-0623	Resident: $25 Nonresident: $120
Conservation Commission	508-759-0625	
Natural Resource Department	508-759-0623	

Town of Brewster

Beach parking permits	508-896-4511	Resident: $6/vehicle Nonresident: $25/week or $8/day/vehicle (purchase at gate)
Shellfish permits	508-896-3701	Resident: $15 Nonresident: $35/week
Conservation Commission	508-896-3701	

Town of Chatham

Beach parking permits	508-945-5180	Resident: $20/vehicle Nonresident: $8/day (purchase at gate)
Conservation Commission	508-945-5176	
Natural Resource Department	508-945-5176	
Harbormaster	508-945-5185	

Town of Dennis

Beach parking permits	508-394-8300	
Shellfish permits	508-394-8300	Resident: $15 Nonresident: $60
Conservation Commission	508-760-6123	
Harbormaster	508-760-6159	

Town of Eastham

| Beach parking permits | 508-240-5972 | Resident: Free
Nonresident: $20/week/
vehicle |
| Shellfish permits | 508-240-5972 | Resident: $10; senior: free
Nonresident: $25 |

Conservation Commission	508-240-5971
Natural Resource Department	508-240-5950
Harbormaster	508-240-5972

Town of Falmouth

Beach parking permits	508-548-8623
Shellfish permits	508-457-2553
Recreation Department	508-457-2567
Conservation Commission	508-548-7611
Natural Resource Department	508-457-2536
Harbormaster	508-457-2550

Town of Harwich

Beach parking permits	508-430-7516	Resident: $15/vehicle Nonresident: $25/vehicle
Shellfish permits	508-430-7516	Resident: $10; senior: $3 Nonresident: $30/season or $15/day
Recreation Department	508-430-7553	
Conservation Commission	508-430-7506	
Harbormaster	508-430-7553	

Town of Mashpee

Beach parking permits	508-539-1400	
Shellfish permits	508-539-1400	Resident: $15 Nonresident: $50
Recreation Department	508-539-1400	
Conservation Commission	508-539-1414	
Natural Resource Department	508-539-1400	
Harbormaster	508-539-1450	

Town of Orleans

| Beach parking permits | 508-240-3700 | Resident: $35/vehicle
Nonresident: do not issue |

Shellfish permits	508-240-3755	Resident: $5 Nonresident: $15
Recreation Department	508-240-3785	
Conservation Commission	508-240-3700	
Harbormaster	508-240-3755	

Town of Sandwich

Beach parking permits	508-888-4910	Resident: $15/vehicle Nonresident: $20/vehicle

Shellfish permits	508-888-4910	Resident: obtain from town
		  of Bourne
		Nonresident: obtain from
		  town of Bourne

Recreation Department	508-888-4361	
Conservation Commission	508-888-4210	
Harbormaster	508-833-0808	

Town of Truro

Beach parking permits	508-349-3635	
Shellfish permits	508-349-3635	

Town of Yarmouth

Beach parking permits	508-398-2231	Resident: $15/vehicle Nonresident: $8/vehicle/day
Shellfish permits	508-398-2231	Resident: $10 Nonresident: $50
Recreation Department	508-398-2231	
Conservation Commission	508-760-4800	
Harbormaster	508-790-3116	

Outfitters and Guides

Cape Cod Coastal Canoe & Kayak
36 Spectacle Pond Drive, East Falmouth, MA 02536; 508-564-4051;
    1-888-226-6393 (in MA)
E-mail: cccanoe@capecod.net; web site: www.capecodcanoekayak.com
Natural history paddling tours

Cape Cod Kayak
5 Cummaquid Road, North Falmouth, MA 02556; 508-540-9377
Web site: www.capecodkayak.com
Rentals and tours

Cape Cod Waterways
Route 28, Dennis, MA 02638; 508-398-0080
Rentals

Eastern Mountain Sports
1513 Iyanough Road, Hyannis, MA 02601; 508-362-8690
Sales and rentals

Goose Hummock Shop
Route 6A, Orleans, MA 02653; 508-255-0455
Sales and rentals

Jack's Boat Rentals
Nickerson State Park, Brewster, MA 02631; 508-896-8556

Off the Coast Kayak
3 Freeman Street, Provincetown, MA 02657; 1-877-PTKayak (1-877-785-2925)
Web site: www.offthecoast kayak.com
Rentals and tours

Paddler's Shop
1 Shipyard Lane, Cataumet, MA 02534; 508-759-0330

Waquoit Kayak
1209 East Falmouth Highway, East Falmouth, MA 02536; 508-548-9722
Web site: www.waquoitkayak.com
Sales, rentals, and tours

Nonprofit Organizations Providing Paddling Tours

Cape Cod Museum of Natural History
Route 6A, Brewster, MA 02631; 508-896-3867; 1-800 479-3867 (in MA)
E-mail: ccmnh@capecod.net; web site: www.capecodnaturalhistory.org

Cape Cod National Seashore Salt Pond Visitor Center
Route 6, Eastham, MA 02642; 508-255-3421
Web site: www.nps.gov

Wellfleet Bay Wildlife Sanctuary
P.O. Box 236 (off West Road), South Wellfleet, MA 02663; 508-349-2615
E-mail: wellfleet@massaudubon.org; web site: www.wellfleetbay.org

Groups and Organizations

Appalachian Mountain Club (AMC)
Southeastern Massachusetts Chapter
Canoeing and kayaking chair: Muriel Thomas (508-428-3593; e-mail:
    mmtctrv@aol.com)
Web site: www.cris.com/~Ndrma/canoe.htm

Local Equipment Suppliers

Billington Sea Watercraft
41 Branch Point Road, Plymouth, MA 02360; 1-800-286-0083
Sales and rentals

Eastern Mountain Sports
1513 Iyanough Road, Hyannis, MA 02601; 508-362-8690
Sales and rentals

Goose Hummock Shop
Route 6A, Orleans, MA 02653; 508-255-0455
Sales and rentals

Harborside Sport and Tackle
56 Scranton Avenue, Falmouth, MA 02540; 508-548-0143
Sales

Paddler's Shop
1 Shipyard Lane, Cataumet, MA 02534; 508-759-0330
Sales and rentals

Sea Sports
309 Iyanough Road, Hyannis, MA 02601; 508-790-1217
Rentals

Waquoit Kayak
1209 East Falmouth Highway, East Falmouth, MA 02536; 508-548-9722
Sales and rentals

Internet Sites of Interest to the Paddler

Paddling Information Sites

The Paddle Trip Exchange Site: www.members.mint.net/rwirth/waterways/
Northeast Paddlers Message Board: www.npmb.com/index.htm
Great Outdoor Recreation Pages: www.gorp.com
Canoeing and Kayaking Info: www.paddlling.net

Professional Organizations

The Professional Paddlesports Organization: www.propaddle.com
American Canoe Association: www.aca-paddler.org
The Paddlesports Industry Resource: www.gopaddle.org
The Wooden Canoe Heritage Association: www.wcha.org

Magazines and Webzines

Paddler magazine: www.paddlermagazine.com
Canoe and Kayak magazine: www.canoekayak.com
Wave Length magazine: www.wavelengthmagazine.com
Paddler's Web: www.mindlink.bc.ca/summit/

Manufacturers

Aquaterra-Perception Kayaks: www.kayaker.com/
Current Designs: www.cdkayak.com/
Dagger Canoe & Kayak: www.dagger.com/dagger/dagger.html
Feathercraft Folding Kayaks: www.Feathercraft.com/
Folboat Folding Kayaks: www.icondata.com/stores/folbot/
Kiwi Kayak: www.kiwikayak.com/
Klepper Folding Kayak: www.klepper.com/
Laughing Loon Custom Canoes & Kayaks: www.laughingloon.com/
Mad River Canoe: www.youcanpaddle.com
Mohawk Canoes: www.mohawkcanoes.com/
Necky Kayaks: necky.com/kayaks.htm
Nova Craft Canoe: www.novacraft.com/
Ocean Kayak: www.oceankayak.com/
Old Town Canoe: www.otccanoe.com/

Scott Canoe: www.midcanscottcanoe.com/
Swift Canoe & Kayak: www.swiftcanoe.com/
Walden Kayaks: www.waldenkayak.com/models.html
Wenonah Canoes: www.wenonah.com/
Wilderness Systems: www.wildsys.com/

Weather and Tide Information

Interactive Weather Information Network from NOAA. This is a link to the Northeast page, which updates every 60 seconds. iwin.nws.noaa.gov/iwin/graphicsversion/main.html

Shore Guide is a tide chart generator for areas along the New England coast. www.shore.net/cgi-bin/tidechart

Suggested Reference Books

Berrick, Stephan. *Crabs of Cape Cod.* Natural History Series No. 3. Cape Cod Museum of Natural History, 1986.

Birding Cape Cod. Cape Cod Bird Club and Massachusetts Audobon Society, 1989.

Brown, Lauren. *Grasses: An Identification Guide.* Houghton Mifflin, 1979.

Field Guide to the Birds of North America, 3rd edition. National Geographic Society, 1999.

Gosner, Kenneth L. *Atlantic Seashore.* Peterson Field Guides. Houghton Mifflin, 1981.

Hinds, Harold R., and Wilfred A. Hathaway. *Wildflowers of Cape Cod.* Chatham Press, 1968.

Lee, Thomas F. *The Seaweed Handbook.* Dover Publications, 1977.

Strahler, Arthur N. *A Geologist's View of Cape Cod.* Parnassus Imprints, 1966.

Tiner, Ralph W. Jr. *A Field Guide to the Coastal Wetland Plants of the Northeastern United States.* University of Massachusetts Press, 1987.

Trull, Peter. *A Guide to the Common Birds of Cape Cod.* Cape Cod Museum of Natural History, 1991.

Zinn, Donald J. *Marine Mollusks of Cape Cod.* Natural History Series No. 2. Cape Cod Museum of Natural History, 1984.